04-14-10

University of Rhode Island
Robert L. Carothers Library
Kingston, R.I. 02881
401-874-2672

Emily C Laferriere
42 Highwood Drive
Coventry, RI 02816

(401) 480-7589

A hold has been placed on the following item by the patron listed above. Please pull this item and forward it to the pick-up location shown below.

John,
as they say in Irish
'Scéal an chait, a piscín'
(the cat's tale is its kitten).
I wonder if the same can be
said of an author and a book?

Iarfhlaith

Broadcasting in Irish

Minority language, radio, television and identity

Iarfhlaith Watson

FOUR COURTS PRESS

Set in 10 on 13 point Janson Text by
Mac Style Ltd, Scarborough, N. Yorkshire for
FOUR COURTS PRESS LTD
7 Malpas Street, Dublin 8, Ireland
e-mail: info@four-courts-press.ie
and in North America
FOUR COURTS PRESS
c/o ISBS, 920 N.E. 58th Avenue, Suite 300, Portland, OR 97213.

A catalogue record for this title
is available from the British Library.

ISBN 1-85182-731-5 hbk
ISBN 1-85182-732-3 pbk

Printed in Great Britain
by MPG Books, Bodmin, Cornwall.

Contents

Foreword

This series, 'Broadcasting and Irish Society', was inaugurated by Bob Collins, the Director-General of Radio Telefís Éireann, in 1999 with an invitation to myself to act as series editor for a number of individual studies of the development of broadcasting in Ireland since 1926, to mark the 75th anniversary of RTÉ.

As a former Chairman of the Media Association of Ireland I am very conscious of the fact that there has been little opportunity for non-*gaeilgeoirí* to discuss issues relating to Irish-language broadcasting. While the European Bureau for Lesser Used Languages has succeeded in making many critics and commentators aware of the fragility and vulnerability of many marginalized languages, the status of the Irish language – and particularly in relation to the most powerful communications medium, broadcasting – has never been adequately explored in respect of the rights of its speakers to communicate, and be communicated with, in what might be termed a 'lesser used' language.

The fact that Ireland had to wait fifty years for its own Irish-language radio service, and for over thirty years for an Irish-language television service, is a tragedy. But the presence of Irish-language programming on the existing radio and television channels merits a detailed study which Dr Iarfhlaith Watson has now provided. Furthermore, Dr Watson's perspective as a sociologist has enabled him to establish a narrative of the ways in which the perceived rights of Irish speakers were explored as the call for specifically Irish-language broadcast media was articulated.

This is a welcome contribution to the discussion of how Irish people express themselves, identify issues, reach decisions, and organize the means and the content of communication. I am sure it will find its place in the international forum where the relation of broadcasting to the larger society, and the needs of smaller societies and cultures, continue to be topics of consuming passion and interest.

Richard Pine
Series Editor

For Bernadette, Éile and Síomha

Preface

Language plays a complex role in society. Not only is it a means of communication, but it is also often employed as an important element of identity. The English language is regularly represented as a neutral international language, when in reality it is far from neutral. Across the globe, language has tended to be a strong marker of national identity and even an indicator of where national borders could be drawn. Similarly, the Irish language has been presented as a symbol of Irishness.

Although language has been divisive in many places and, like many symbols of identity, has been used to justify conflict, none the less, it is a less exclusive marker of difference. It is less exclusive than markers such as race or even religion. It is not possible to change one's genetic make-up to join another race and it is unusual (at least in this part of the world) to practise more than one religion concurrently, but it is possible to speak several languages.

Language can be a repository of cultural wealth. It can help structure the way we view the world, and the environment in which we live can, in its turn, help structure the language we speak. Although it may no longer be the case that the Irish language holds any unique cultural treasures, it is a cultural treasure in its own right. After independence the Irish State took it upon itself to restore the Irish language and although it has not achieved that objective, it has managed to maintain a significant number of Irish speakers. The education system played a role in this. The State also tried to employ radio and later television in this operation, but with less success. That Irish-language television can facilitate the restoration of Irish is doubtful, but it provides Irish speakers and others with entertainment and information in Irish.

This book is the result of a lengthy period of research from 1993 to 2002. During 1993–9 the main focus of my research was the Irish-language television channel. This became the subject of a manuscript which I submitted to Four Courts Press. By a happy coincidence Richard Pine had been commissioned with putting together a series of books under the title 'Broadcasting and Irish Society' to celebrate seventy-five years of broadcasting in Ireland 1926–2001. I was delighted that he felt that the series needed a book covering the seventy-five years of broadcasting in Irish and I conducted further research to expand and restructure my manuscript to suit this series.

As a sociologist I didn't want to provide a description of broadcasting in Irish without some kind of analysis and yet, at the same time, I didn't want to present a purely sociological analysis. I brought the two sides together by employing the well-known concept 'national identity'. I argue that the Irish language plays an important role in national identity and I attempt to illustrate how changes in broadcasting in Irish coincide with changes in national identity.

Thanks are due to a number of people, in no particular order: Bernadette Ryan, whose hard work kept us both above the emotional and financial poverty line; Dr Máire Nic Ghiolla Phádraig, who gave exactly the right advice; my parents for their evident example; Richard Pine for spotting the potential in a much earlier draft and for providing useful comments on a later draft; RTÉ for supporting this series of books; Professor Stephen Mennell for providing me with many opportunities to practise my 'craft'; the various people who gave generously of their time: Dr Michael D. Higgins TD, Ciarán Ó Feinneadha, Donncha Ó hÉalaithe, Nollag Ó Gadhra, Colm Ó Briain and especially Pádhraic Ó Ciardha, as well as unnamed civil servants; Dr Elihu Katz for his helpful comments and providing me with the opportunity to test some of my ideas at the American Sociological Association Conference in Toronto, 1997. I can't forget the helpful comments over coffee, in various offices, at lunchtime seminars, etc., or even the occasional throw-away remark from amongst others: Dónal Griffin, Dr Steven Loyal, Dr Bryan Fanning, Mick Rush, Martin Ryan, Professor Eric Dunning, Professor Tom Garvin, Rónán Ó Dúnáin, Dr Sara O'Sullivan, Margaret O'Keeffe, Stephen Ryan, Bernie Grummel, Paul Ryan, Ciarán Staunton, Eoin O'Mahony, Anne Cleary, Aoife Rickard, Jessica Bates, Dr Ian Cornelius, John Steele, Dr Don Bennett, Dr Tom Inglis and Dr Mary Kelly for helping me get started in the first place, and the various other members of the Department of Sociology, UCD; and special thanks to Catherine Baulch for helping me out when I was short on time. My apologies if I have overlooked anybody.

A chronology of ministers responsible for broadcasting

Postmasters-General (1921–4), Ministers for Posts and Telegraphs (1924–84), for Communications (1984–94) and for Broadcasting (1994–7)[1]

1st Dáil (21 January 1919–1 April 1919): None.

2nd Dáil (26 August 1921–9 January 1922): James J. Walsh (as Postmaster-General).

3rd Dáil (9 September 1922–9 August 1923): James J. Walsh.

4th Dáil (19 September 1923–23 May 1927): James J. Walsh (becoming Minister for Posts and Telegraphs from 2 June 1924 under the Ministers and Secretaries Act, 1924)

5th Dáil (23 June 1927–25 August 1927): James J. Walsh.

6th Dáil (11 October 1927–29 January 1932): Ernest Blythe.

7th Dáil (9 March 1932–2 January 1933): Joseph Connolly.

8th Dáil (8 February 1933–14 June 1937): Gerald Boland to 11 November 1936; Oscar Traynor, 11 November 1936–.

9th Dáil (21 July 1937–27 May 1938): Oscar Traynor.

10th Dáil (30 June 1938–26 June 1943): Oscar Traynor to 8 September 1939; Patrick Little, 8 September 1939–.

11th Dáil (1 July 1943–7 June 1944): Patrick Little.

12th Dáil (9 June 1944–12 January 1948): Patrick Little.

13th Dáil (18 February 1948–7 May 1951): James Everett.

14th Dáil (13 June 1951–24 May 1954): Erskine Childers.

15th Dáil (2 June 1954–12 February 1957): Michael Keyes.

16th Dáil (20 March 1957–15 September 1961): Neil Blaney to 4 December 1957; John Ormonde, 4 December 1957–24 June 1959; Michael Hilliard 24 June 1959–.

---

1 Source: www.antaoiseach.ie

17th Dáil (11 October 1961–18 March 1965): Michael Hilliard.

18th Dáil (21 April 1965–22 May 1969): Joseph Brennan to 10 November 1966; Erskine Childers, 10 November 1966–.

19th Dáil (18 June 1969–5 February 1973): Patrick J. Lalor to 9 May 1970; Gerard Collins, 9 May 1970–.

20th Dáil (14 March 1973–25 May 1977): Conor Cruise O'Brien.

21st Dáil (5 July 1977–21 May 1981): Padraig Faulkner to 11 December 1979; Albert Reynolds, 11 December 1979–.

22nd Dáil (30 June 1981–27 January 1982): Patrick Cooney.

23rd Dáil (9 March 1982–14 December 1982): John P. Wilson.

24th Dáil (14 December 1982–21 January 1987): Jim Mitchell (Minister for Communications from 2 January 1984).

25th Dáil (10 March 1987–25 May 1989): John P. Wilson to 31 March 1987; Ray Burke from 31 March 1987.

26th Dáil (12 July 1989–5 November 1992): Ray Burke to 6 February 1991; Seamus Brennan 6 February 1991–11 February 1992 (becoming Minister for Tourism, Transport and Communications from 7 February 1991); Maire Geoghegan-Quinn from 11 February 1992.

27th Dáil (14 December 1992–15 May 1997): Michael D. Higgins (as Minister for Arts, Culture and the Gaeltacht he also had responsibility for broadcasting).

28th Dáil (28 June 1997–24 April 2002): Síle de Valera (as Minister for Arts, Culture and the Gaeltacht, including broadcasting).

29th Dáil (20 June 2002 to date): Dermot Ahern (as Minister for Communications, Marine and Natural Resources).

CHAPTER 1

Introduction: Irish-language broadcasting and national identity

'The regular transmission of a song or a play in the national language will be a powerful factor in the creation of a national being'.[1] Thus spoke Richard Hayward (a writer from Northern Ireland) in 1925. That short sentence contains three aspects, which are at the centre of this book. These are the Irish language, broadcasting and national identity. All three are interrelated and the relationship between them has changed continually in the intervening three-quarters of a century. The importance of these three factors was relatively new to the recently independent Irish State of the 1920s. The aim of reviving Irish had emerged in the late nineteenth century, was reinforced by the establishment of the Gaelic League in 1892 and was institutionalised by the Irish State after 1922. Radio was a new invention and the first radio channels began broadcasting in the early 1920s. With regard to national identity, this was of particular importance for the new State.

After independence, and especially after the civil war, the Irish State found it necessary to rebuild the nation, both physically and socially. The physical reconstruction of buildings and roads was important to the fledgling State, but even more important was to bring the people together. The war of independence and the civil war had created divisions within Irish society. National identity brought a shared sense of belonging to the majority of the population. This sense of belonging also justified the existence of the State, independent of the United Kingdom, and helped to forge a national community.

At the turn of the century, from the nineteenth to the twentieth, many new nation-states emerged in Europe. This was the era in which many of the national identities and nationalisms of Europe were conceived.[2] Irish national identity emerged in the context of that *zeitgeist* (spirit of the age). Although, Irish national identity, and the other European national identities that

---

1 Richard Hayward quoted in R. Cathcart, 'Broadcasting – the early decades' in Brian Farrell (ed.), *Communications and community in Ireland* (Dublin: Mercier Press, 1984), p. 42.   2 Cf. E. Hobsbawm, *Nations and nationalism since 1780* (Cambridge: Cambridge University Press, 1990) for an indepth analysis of the nation-building process of the time.

1

emerged during that era, have changed in the intervening century, an insight into that era helps us to understand some of the strands of those identities that have remained and have influenced events at the turn of this century.

Identity is an extremely complex issue. It is presented as natural and pre-existing, but our national identity is neither the same now as it was in the 1920s, nor was it the same in the 1920s as it had been before then. The sense of identity that emerged in Ireland from the late nineteenth century was based on the resources of history – reviving and creating traditions that would make that identity seem natural and pre-existing. Identity is constructed and exists socially; in other words it is constructed by people and exists within and between them. National identity brings individuals together as a nation and just as national borders mark the boundary between nation-states, identity marks the boundary between 'us' and 'them'. Some of the key elements of the Irish national identity of a century ago demonstrate that the boundary being marked was the one between Irishness and Britishness. Of central importance to that sense of identity was that the Irish were different from the British and were therefore entitled to national self-determination. The differences high-lighted were differences of religion, of sports, of economic base and of lan-guage, as well as others. Even if all Irish people were not Catholic, were not members of the GAA (Gaelic Athletic Association), did not live and work in the countryside and could not speak Irish, at least these could be presented as common features and held as symbols of a shared identity.

National identity is also an ideology. It is a shared set of beliefs and symbols. It is not just about ideas the actions that manifest the shared beliefs are also relevant. Crucially, the term ideology refers to the way these symbols and beliefs intersect with relations of power.[3] The new Irish national identity reinforced the power and legitimacy of the new State and the new elite that replaced the earlier British power holders. The new leaders did not have to speak Irish, no more than the general population did, but they recognised its symbolic importance. What this meant was that they would use key phrases in the rituals of government and promote its revival and its use in daily life and in broadcasting.

Radio broadcasting came into existence at a very convenient time for the new Irish State. Some politicians and civil servants saw in it the potential to dis-seminate and reinforce Irish identity. To a large extent even radio itself was a symbol of difference – not only did the nation have its own language, reli-gion etc., it also had its own radio station. As well as its symbolic importance radio was a medium that could be used to create a shared sense of belonging.

---

3 Cf. J.B. Thompson, 'Ideology and modern culture' in A. Giddens, D. Held, D. Hubert, D. Seymore and J. Thompson (eds), *The polity reader in social theory* (Cambridge: Polity Press, 1994), particularly p. 135 for a discussion of a more critical, as opposed to passive, conceptualisation of ideology.

This is manifested in the programmes broadcast. Irish songs and songs in Irish, dances[4] and GAA games were broadcast. These were symbols of Irish identity. It was not the singing of the songs, the playing of the games or the speaking of the language that was important, but that they were sung, played and spoken by somebody. Broadcasting in Irish was a symbolic act, marking the difference between the Irish, who own this language, and others. Even broadcasting programmes for learners was more symbolic than constructive.

The symbolic importance of Irish on radio was clear from the start of broadcasting in Ireland. On 1 January 1926 2RN (misunderstood by some to mean 'to Erin')[5] began broadcasting from Dublin. This was the first domestic radio station. Douglas Hyde (founder of the Gaelic League) was invited to give the inaugural speech. In that speech he emphasised the importance of Irish for creating an Irish nation. The Postmaster-General (James J. Walsh)[6] spoke in the Dáil 'of the need for a Gaeltacht'[8] radio service. There were broadcasts in Irish on 2RN and on the more national Radio Éireann that came later. While the amount of time devoted to broadcasting in Irish was relatively small, it was of symbolic importance.

Irish was a central prop of national identity. Many of the other new nation states similarly held language to be an important feature of their national identity. Their political leaders' claims, of the nation's right to self-determination, were based on the nation's shared language. From this perspective it was important that the Irish could claim that they had their own language.

Even after independence the existence of Irish continued to be of symbolic importance, but, for some, it was necessary to move beyond the symbolism, particularly with the support of the new State. It was hoped that Irish could be revived as the spoken language of Ireland. To achieve this, Irish was introduced as a compulsory component of the school curriculum and gradually the State also made knowledge of Irish compulsory for promotion within and entrance to the civil service and for entrance to the National University of Ireland. The manner in which the language was imposed on the people is a reflection of the time. The State was building the nation. It had a vision of how the nation should be, and made efforts to construct that nation.

National identity reflected that ideal. It was a social, almost communal model. Irish political leaders presented the Irish people as if they all shared

---

4 Strange as it sounds, Irish dances on radio were quite popular. Presumably their popularity came from the popularity of dance music generally.   5 Cf. R. Pine, *2RN and the origins of Irish radio* (Dublin: Four Courts Press, 2002), also in this series.   6 James J. Walsh was Postmaster-General and Minister for Posts and Telegraphs, 1921–7.   7 The lower legislative, representative house of parliament. It translates as 'Assembly'.   8 The Gaeltacht is an appellation employed to describe certain geographical areas containing a diverse group of communities that are predominantly Irish-speaking. These communities are mainly in the West of Ireland, including areas in Counties Cork and Kerry (south-west), County Galway (west), Counties Mayo and Donegal (north-west), but also including a small community in County Meath (mid-east) and in County Waterford (south-east).

the same beliefs and, if they didn't, it was the State's role to socialise them appropriately – to make them all speak Irish, for example. The national identity of those early years is not the same as we have now, but in order to categorise and illustrate the changes I will divide the twentieth century into three eras in which Irish national identity had distinct characteristics and coincided with developments in broadcasting. The national identity of the first few decades after independence could be called 'traditional', because it drew on and constructed traditions and made it seem that this national identity was a continuation from the past.[9]

The State wanted to protect its fledgling nation both culturally and economically from outside influences. The economic regime of the 1930s–1950s was protectionist and reflected the cultural regime of the time. The shared identity was based on having a different religion, language etc. from others, particularly the British. Irish radio had a role to play in attracting listeners away from 'foreign' broadcasts and protecting the Irish from their influence and at the same time disseminating Irish identity by including the symbols of that identity.

By the 1950s it was clear that the nationalist aims of the earlier nation-building project had not been achieved. Economic protectionism, as well as its cultural form, had failed. For example, economically the country was in dire straits, emigration was high, the State could not provide sufficient employment; culturally, Irish had not become the language of the people. It was at this time that certain academics, civil servants and politicians launched an ideological offensive to liberalise Irish economy and society.[10] Emerging from this was a project of modernisation. The aim was to modernise the Irish economy and an important element of this was the modernisation of beliefs.[11] The State started to open the Irish economy and society to influences outside its borders.

The main feature of the era was liberalisation. This can be discerned in both economics and culture during the 1960s and 1970s. In relation to Irish there was a slight liberalisation in education; for example, from the early 1970s it was no longer necessary to receive at least a pass grade in Irish in order to pass the Leaving Certificate. In 1964 the Language Freedom Movement was established, advocating the elimination of the compulsory nature of Irish in the education system and in the civil service. Freedom of

9 Cf. A. Gramsci, *Selections from the Prison Notebooks* (London: Lawrence and Wishart, 1971) for an obscure discussion of the role of the traditional intelligentsia. 10 Cf. L. O'Dowd, 'State legitimacy and nationalism in Ireland' in P. Clancy et al. (eds), *Ireland and Poland: comparative perspectives* (Dublin: Department of Sociology, University College Dublin, 1992), p. 33. 11 Cf. A. Webster, *Introduction to the sociology of development* (London: Macmillan Press, 1990, 2nd edn) or P. Kirby, *Poverty amid plenty: world and Irish development reconsidered* (Dublin: Trócaire, 1997) for a general discussion of modernisation theory or J.J. Lee, *Ireland 1912–1985: politics and society* (Cambridge: Cambridge University Press, 1989) for a discussion of the modernisation of Ireland.

choice was important to this group and was also a trait of the emerging ideology. This freedom of choice was reflected in the term 'rights'. The 1960s was the era of mass social movements across the Western World, most of these social movements were based on rights.

This ideology was economistic and individualistic. At its centre was the rational individual. This individual was thought to have rights as a consumer. Economically the consumer should be provided with a range of choices. These choices would be in competition with one another and the 'best' product would 'win'. This ideology was evident in the cultural sphere as well – again 'consumers' would have a range of choices and the most popular choice would 'win'. This was also the case for the symbols of national identity – people should be allowed to choose the sport they played, the religion they practised and the language they spoke, without any one having a monopoly. This had a double implication for Irish broadcasting. Listeners and viewers had the choice of tuning in to programmes in Irish; however, if a sufficient number did not tune in, that programme was deemed uneconomic – to have lost the competition. Many, if not most, programmes in Irish did not achieve the same ratings as their equivalents in English. This is to be expected as only 5 or 10% of people in Ireland speak Irish with relative fluency.

Television began in Ireland at the beginning of this period of modernisation and liberalisation. It began under the new structure of the RTÉ[12] Authority, which was established in the Broadcasting Authority Act, 1960. This new structure itself was a child of the new ideology insofar as it was a liberalisation of broadcasting by making it more independent of State control. The new ideology was manifest in the operation of RTÉ. There was an increasing emphasis on achieving the highest possible ratings for television programmes. This illustrated a shift from the earlier nation-building ideology, in which the State influenced programmes in a direction that would mould listeners in the image of the traditional national identity, to a new ideology, in which the type of programmes that were most popular would survive. That is not to say that broadcasters had not been interested in the popularity of their programmes, far from it, but there has been a particular emphasis on ratings since the arrival of television. Moreover, less popular, but symbolically important, programmes have continued to be broadcast, but the emphasis on ratings and the low ratings of such programmes has tended to undermine their acceptability.

The national identity that emerged during the 1960s tended to disregard the nationalistic nation-building symbols of the traditional national identity and to emphasise instead the modernisation project. The emphasis on

---

12 Radio Telefís Éireann, which translates as 'Radio Television [of] Ireland', is the Irish public broadcasting service.

economics in Ireland reflected the move in Europe towards economic unification and the de-emphasis of national differences. This movement in
Europe was toward economic unification in an effort to move away from the
nationalist tendencies which had contributed to the two world wars. In
Ireland, however, the considerable intensification of conflict in Northern
Ireland brought the nationalist characteristics of the traditional national
identity into focus. The result was a shift within the modern ideology from
disregarding the symbols of the earlier national identity to a concerted effort
to de-emphasise them.

By the 1970s, although the traditional national identity was still very
much in evidence in the beliefs of Irish people, and its symbols were ubiqui-
tous, a 'modern' element was entering national identity. This emerging
national identity was based on individual choices and individual rights.
Individuals were expected to choose their identity rationally and could draw
on a variety of beliefs and symbols that were acceptable in Irish identity.
According to the modern ideology, individuals had the right to choose their
identity, which they would construct from a range of equally valid beliefs and
symbols, and they would make this choice rationally. This differed from the
earlier traditional ideology in which national identity was inflexible and was
imposed on the nation as a whole.

In the Gaeltacht in the late 1960s this new ideology was employed by
Gluaiseacht Cearta Sibhialta na Gaeltachta (the Gaeltacht Civil Rights
Movement) to argue that they had the right to a radio station in the language
they chose to speak. Raidió na Gaeltachta[13] emerged and began broadcasting
in 1972. Also as the mass-conversion of pupils to Irish had not succeeded and
the efforts were being regarded with disdain, the Gaelscoileanna (Irish-
language schools) increased in number offering parents the choice of having
their children educated in Irish.

Later in the 1970s English speakers in Ireland were also using the language of rights to demand more choice from television broadcasting. People
who lived beyond the footprint'[14] of the BBC were demanding the right to
more television channels. Those who lived on the east coast or near the
border with Northern Ireland could receive BBC broadcasts from the air.
The debate began about a second Irish television channel.[15] Originally the
objective was to rebroadcast BBC to the rest of the country. The Irish-language movement argued that a second channel would provide more airtime
in which to increase the amount of broadcasting in Irish. The channel that
emerged was a second channel for RTÉ and was expected to be used mainly

---

13 Raidió na Gaeltachta or RnaG is the Gaeltacht radio channel, which can be received outside the
Gaeltacht as well.   **14** By 'footprint' I mean the area within which the broadcasts could be received.
15 See Muiris Mac Conghail's forthcoming book on the second channel, in this series.

to broadcast imported programmes. The arrival of RTÉ2 in 1979 provided choice in television viewing and opened Ireland up even more to outside influences.

During the 1970s the Irish-language movement, based in Dublin, as well as its Gaeltacht equivalent continued to demand an increase in programmes in Irish on RTÉ television. By the 1980s a Gaeltacht group began to demand a separate television channel in Irish. The arguments for more Irish on RTÉ and for a separate channel in Irish were both based on the modern ideology of rights. The logic behind the argument was that individual rights in the context of competition tended to result in the majority gaining their rights to the detriment of the minority. This would mean that only the beliefs and symbols chosen by the majority would 'win'. Irish was in a difficult position because, for the majority of the population, it was purely symbolic – they wanted it to exist and were sympathetic of a limited support for it in education, broadcasting etc., but could not speak it and would not watch programmes in Irish on television. The individual-rights argument would disadvantage all minorities in Ireland. The argument for an increase in television broadcasting in Irish was based on a minority-rights position, which claimed that it is the right of those who choose to speak Irish to be informed and entertained in that language.

By the early 1990s there were signs that a separate Irish-language television channel would be established. After a national campaign by a pressure group, all the political parties adopted it in their manifestos. After important interventions by two ministers in the early-to-mid-1990s, a separate Irish-language television channel began broadcasting in 1996. This channel emerged in a context in which the liberal ideology had moved forward and was now more neoliberal. The State opened up beyond Europe to more global influences. The neoliberal ideology meant a further individualisation of identity and of economy. In the Celtic-Tiger era the new Irish-language television channel (TnaG)[16] seeks its share of the national audience (unlike RnaG, which had a Gaeltacht community-based audience). In the increasingly individualised environment in the four decades since television began in Ireland the audience has been regarded less and less as an homogeneous, or even segmented national whole. Furthermore, the arrival of new television channels over the decades and recent developments in digital television are leading toward a further fragmentation of television channels.

RTÉ and its programmes in Irish face the full shock of this fragmentation. Although TnaG is protected to some extent by support from RTE and financial support from the Government, it is also affected to some extent by the

---

16 The channel was initially called Teilifís na Geilge (TnaG), but was relaunched as TG4 in 1999.

individualisation of identity and the fragmentation of viewing. None the less, it has managed to find a niche for itself and continues to grow. RnaG is shielded by having a clear niche within the Gaeltacht and being funded by RTÉ. Although it has been affected by competition with community and local commercial radio channels, it is sheltered. RnaG has been highly praised over the decades and has continued to hold its own within the Gaeltacht and reach out beyond.

CHAPTER 2

Early years: the role of Irish on 2RN and Radio Éireann

Broadcasting in Ireland, including broadcasting in Irish, has come a long way since the 1920s and yet an understanding of those early years is vital to our appreciation of the current context. An awareness of the society of the time is also crucial because broadcasting exists in, is shaped by, and influences society. In this chapter information is presented about the historical development of Irish broadcasting and broadcasting in Irish during the first three or four decades after independence. After the war of independence and the civil war, national cohesion was important for stability and the legitimation of the new State. Fundamental to that national cohesion was a version of Irish national identity that placed the Irish language at the centre. The State promoted this identity by including its various elements, such as the Irish language, in broadcasting.

GENERAL EFFORTS TO PRESERVE AND RESTORE
THE IRISH LANGUAGE

Background to the Irish language
Irish, as a minority language, has a relatively large number of speakers and has a state to support it. The EU (European Union) is multilingual, most member-states contain at least one autochthonous[1] language and there are, moreover, several official languages of the EU. There is a distinct difference, however, between languages such as French, German or English and languages such as Irish, Welsh, Basque or Catalan in that the former languages do not require 'support' and 'protection'. There is one apparent dissimilarity between Irish and the other minority languages – Irish has an independent state to 'support' and 'protect' it. Nonetheless, according to the renowned sociolinguist Joshua Fishman, governments and various organisations 'often

---

1 Autochthonous literally means 'from that place', but in this context it implies original and minority.

find that independence is not enough to guarantee ethnocultural and ethno-linguistic distinctiveness and find it necessary, therefore, to institute "cultural policies" and "language policies"[2] and, in the case of Ireland, even these are sometimes insufficient.

It may be claimed, according to the Irish-language activist Desmond Fennell, that 'when the Irish State was established in 1922 … its two principle cultural aims were to revive Irish in English-speaking Ireland and to "save the Gaeltacht".'[3] Following from this, one can discern several motives for the institution of language policies in Ireland since independence. The most self-evident is the link that has been perceived to exist between national identity and Irish. As Tovey, Hannon and Abramson claimed, 'it is the widespread use of our own language that provides the most effective basis for any valid claims to membership of a distinctive peoplehood'.[4] This argument existed before independence and became a principle of national identity. This was also argued by the CLAR (Committee on Irish Language Attitudes Research) report (1975) which claimed that the fundamental manifestation of an 'Irish' worldview[5] locates the Irish language in a position as 'validator of our cultural distinctiveness'.[6]

The Irish language has been an important element of national identity since before independence. One finds that attitudes to the language are considerably positive; for example, 41.2% of the population of Ireland returned themselves as Irish speakers in the most recent census (1996) (1,430,205 individuals). This has increased dramatically over the last few censuses. It is an indication, however, of a positive attitude, rather than linguistic ability. This positive attitude stems from the position of Irish within national identity, so that even people who cannot speak Irish regard it as an element of their national identity. Figures for ability, on the other hand, are unclear, but it appears, from various surveys undertaken by Institiúid Teangeolaíochta Éireann (ITÉ – the Linguistics Institute of Ireland), that at most 10% of the population of Ireland can engage in conversations in Irish. Perhaps only half of those do so regularly. Another survey by ITÉ found that 2% of the population is native speaking and a further 9% with fluent or near-fluent ability.[7]

The heartland of Irish is the Gaeltacht and its survival is of symbolic importance for national identity. Most, if not all, native speakers probably

---

2 J. Fishman, *Reversing language shift: theoretical and empirical foundations of assistance to threatened languages* (Clevedon: Multilingual Matters, 1991), pp. 27–8.   **3** D. Fennell, 'Can a shrinking linguistic minority be saved? Lessons from the Irish experience' in Einar Haugen et al. (eds), *Minority languages today* (Edinburgh: Edinburgh University Press, 1980), p. 33.   **4** H. Tovey, D. Hannan and H. Abramson, *Why Irish? Irish identity and the Irish language* (Dublin: Bord na Gaeilge, 1989), p. iii.   **5** World View is the outlook on the world of an individual or a specific social group. The original German term is *Weltanschauung*.   **6** The Advisory Planning Committee, *The Irish language in a changing society: shaping the future* (Dublin: Bord na Gaeilge, 1986) p. 61.   **7** P. Ó Riagáin and M. Ó Gliasáin, *National survey on languages 1993: preliminary report* (Dublin: ITÉ, 1994).

live, or were brought up, in the Gaeltacht. The Gaeltacht population contains 2.4% of the entire population of the country; however, 22.9% of the Gaeltacht population are not Irish speakers, thus, according to the 1996 census, Irish speakers living in the Gaeltacht account for 1.75% of the population of Ireland. In terms of the numbers, there are approximately eighty thousand (82,715) people living in the Gaeltacht and approximately sixty thousand (61,035) of them are Irish speakers (including migrants with school Irish). However, the vast majority of Irish speakers do not live in, or come from, the Gaeltacht. These Irish speakers are, by and large, the result of state efforts to restore the language.[8]

Restoration: Irish-language policy and the education system
The language policy which was adopted by the Government in the early 1920s was directly influenced by the work of the Gaelic League (established in 1893) in endeavouring to restore Irish. The government policy was to assign Irish to a significant position in the new school curricula. Since independence, the language policy of the Government has been mainly located in the restoration of the language through the education system, which, according to Tovey et al. has meant that 'we have left the really important elements of our identity in the hands of elites and experts, and they have returned them to us as doctrines externally imposed'.[9] The concluding few words of this statement express a sentiment which has become a common experience for many people in Ireland – the Irish language as taught in school is one tenet of an overall doctrine, alien to the experiences of the pupils and imposed against their will.

The encounter between pupils and Irish at school has left many pupils unsympathetic to the condition of the language and according to Peillon 'many people deny that a privileged relationship exists between the Irish language and national identity'.[10] Nonetheless, it seems that within a few years of leaving school most people have established an attachment to the language, as was evinced by the CLAR survey[11] (conducted in 1973) and by the ITÉ follow-up surveys in 1983 and 1993, which found that for most respondents Irish occupies a central role in national identity. These surveys also suggest that there is a trend towards less negative and more positive views of the Irish language.

The language policy which introduced compulsory Irish to the education system was primarily a policy of restoration, insofar as it was an attempt to

8 Oifig an tSoláthair, *Daonáireamh 86, Imleabhar 5: An Ghaeilge* (Baile Átha Cliath: Oifig Dhíolta Foilseacháin Rialtais, 1993): Stationery Office, *Census 86, Issue 5: Irish* (Dublin: Government Stationery Office, 1993). **9** H. Tovey et al., op. cit., p. 21. **10** M. Peillon, *Contemporary Irish society: an introduction* (Dublin: Gill and Macmillan, 1982), p. 101. **11** CLAR, *Committee on Irish Language Attitudes research report* (Dublin: Government Stationery Office, 1975).

expand the Irish-speaking population. This effort of restoration has worked to maintain and to some extent increase the number of Irish speakers in the Galltacht (the rest of Ireland, outside the Gaeltacht Irish-speaking communities). Unfortunately, the reproduction of Irish speakers depends primarily on the school system rather than on family or community and, according to Pádraig Ó Riagáin from ITÉ, 'were it not for the fact that the schools continue to produce a small but committed percentage of bilinguals, the maintenance of this small minority of Irish speakers would long since have failed';[12] so, future changes in the educational system may affect this reproduction.

Preservation: Irish-language policy and the Gaeltacht
Another part of the language policy of the Government has been the preservation of the language in the traditionally Irish-speaking Gaeltacht areas. One of the main causes of decrease in the numbers of Irish speakers in these areas is demographic. Both inward and outward migration can have a detrimental effect on a language. In the case of the Gaeltacht, the decrease in the number of Irish speakers was primarily seen as the product of emigration, thus the policy for the Gaeltacht was to stem the tide of emigration through economic policies. As the Minister for the Gaeltacht said in 1975, 'No jobs, no people; no people, no Gaeltacht; no Gaeltacht, no language.'[13] As a policy for reversing the decline of the Gaeltacht population it worked adequately – in 1971 the population of the Gaeltacht was 70,568 and this rose to 79,502 by 1981.[14] As a language policy it had drastic consequences, however, because these figures conceal the continuing trend of emigration among the young Gaeltacht population. As the increased employment in the secondary and tertiary sectors caused immigration of better qualified non-Gaeltacht or returning-emigrant workers (usually with a non-Gaeltacht spouse), the young people from the Gaeltacht were still forced to emigrate. The result was that, although the population increased, the percentage of Irish speakers in the Gaeltacht decreased (82.9% of the Gaeltacht population was Irish-speaking in 1971 in comparison with 77.4% in 1981).[15] The decrease in the proportion of Irish speakers to non-Irish speakers can cause an accelerating rate of decline in the number of Irish speakers, as the increased numbers of non-Irish speakers are incorporated into the community. (The presence of even one non-Irish speaker in a group of Irish speakers 'obliges' the (bilingual) Irish speakers to speak English). A reduction in the ratio of Irish speakers to non-Irish speakers in a predominantly Irish-speaking community, which had

12 P. Ó Riagáin, 'Introduction', *Language Planning in Ireland: International Journal of the Sociology of Language*, 70 (1988), p. 7.   13 Quoted in P. Commins, 'Socioeconomic development and language maintenance in the Gaeltacht', ibid., p. 14.   14 The Advisory Planning Committee, op. cit., pp. 1–2.
15 J. Fishman, op. cit., p. 124.

a stable percentage of Irish speakers, can introduce decline. This has added significance when one considers that 'the [CLAR] report postulated that a critical mass of at least 80% of the people of a community with high ability levels was necessary to maintain a stable diglossic situation'.[16] In some Gaeltacht communities more than 80% of the population had been Irish-speaking up to the mid-1970s. Young, unskilled Irish speakers continued to leave the Gaeltacht to find employment. From the mid-1970s these young emigrants were replaced by skilled non-Irish-speaking workers and families availing of the opportunity of employment provided by the Government's industrialisation of the Gaeltacht. This caused a decrease in the percentage of Irish speakers to less than 80% and introduced a continuing decline in the Irish language in these communities.

Restoration and preservation: a conclusion
The policies of restoration and preservation have been general and unfocused. They were manifested in the education system and in the industrialisation of the Gaeltacht respectively. Fishman claimed that in Ireland

> There has been a surfeit of Governmental bureaucracy and monopolisation of support or control, but ... local voluntary efforts are often in a better position to achieve breakthroughs than are ponderous, costly, centrally controlled, nationwide efforts.[17]

Similarly, Peillon argued that 'the taking up of the cause of revival by the State and its consequent institutionalisation might turn out to be the kiss of death to the rich reservoir of the gaelic heritage'.[18] On that point Fishman 'counsels greater sociocultural self-sufficiency, self-help, self-regulation and initiative at the "lower level", so to speak, before seriously pursuing such "higher level" arenas'.[19] Fishman proposed what he called a 'Graded Intergenerational Disruption Scale', in which he set out eight stages for reversing language shift. The achievement of each stage rests upon the accomplishments of the previous stage(s). According to this scale the intergenerational transmission of the language (stage six) is the crucial stage and has not been adequately achieved in Ireland – first, the declining number of Irish speakers in the Gaeltacht is evidence that the language is not being transmitted from generation to generation and, second, the reproduction of the language through the education system, which manifests a certain measure of achievement, is dependent on the State rather than on family or community. His final stage, once all the other stages have been achieved, is nationwide broadcasting in the language.

16 P. Commins, op. cit., p. 23.   **17** J. Fishman, op. cit., p. 142.   **18** M. Peillon, op. cit., pp. 104–5.
19 J. Fishman, op. cit., p. 4.

USING RADIO TO PRESERVE AND RESTORE IRISH

During the early years of the State, Irish music, sports, language and religion (Catholicism) were to be heard on radio. These were central elements of national identity. It will be argued below that one of the functions reserved for radio was the promotion of national identity and national distinctiveness. This function could be served by broadcasting programmes which reflected this national identity. Some listeners, politicians and civil servants argued, however, that these were programmes to which the State felt the people *should* listen, not necessarily programmes to which the people *wanted* to listen. They presented the State's worldview, i.e. its view of the nation, of the rest of the world and of the nation's position in the world. On this point the Postmaster-General (and soon thereafter retitled Minister for Posts and Telegraphs) of the time (i.e. 1924) said:

> We ... claim that this nation has set out on a separate existence. That existence not only covers its political life, but also its social and cultural life, and I take it to be a part of the fight which this nation has made during the last six or seven years that this separate entity should not only be gripped but developed to the utmost until this country is prop-erly set on its feet as an independent, self-thinking, self-supporting nation in every respect ... Any kind of Irish station is better than no Irish station at all.[20]

The Postmaster-General also pointed to the negative affect on the restoration of the Irish language if Irish people could only hear British broadcasts. Similarly, Mary Kelly claimed that 'since the establishment of the state the national broadcasting service has been important in symbolically elaborating Irish national identity and cultural difference'.[21] These authors and others have argued that radio was employed as a tool to assist in the construction of an Irish nation. Not only was broadcasting important for disseminating national identity, but the Irish language was central to this.

Maurice Gorham, who was Director of Broadcasting in Radio Éireann 1953–60, gave an informative account of radio broadcasting up to the midsix-ties.[22] He began his history of broadcasting in Ireland in 1916. On Easter Monday 1916 rebels occupied the Irish School of Wireless Telegraphy on the

---

20 *First, Second and Third Interim Reports and the Final Report of the Special Committee to Consider the Wireless Broadcasting Report together with Proceedings of the Committees, Minutes of Evidence and Appendices* (Dublin: Stationery Office, 1924). para. 389.   **21** M. Kelly, 'The media and national identity in Ireland' in Patrick Clancy et al. (eds), op. cit., p. 79.   **22** M. Gorham, *Forty years of broadcasting* (Dublin: Talbot Press, 1967), p. 2.

corner of O'Connell Street and Lower Abbey Street in Dublin, but because of sniper fire from British soldiers they could not get the aerial on the roof and the transmitter into operation until the next day and because of artillery fire the transmitter had to be moved to the General Post Office on O'Connell Street the following day. In 1916 the only transmission possible, however, was using morse code, none the less, the rebels managed to transmit a message on the shipping frequency to whomsoever could receive it – this method of transmitting, to everybody who is willing and able to receive, is called 'broadcasting'. The broadcast consisted of news that an Irish Republic had been declared. This early broadcast was a sign of what was to come after independence.

Ireland was a little later than other countries in broadcasting speech and music because of the civil war (1920–3). Although the civil war ended in May 1923, the Postmaster-General (J.J. Walsh) had prepared a White Paper on broadcasting as early as November 1923, and then in early 1924 the Special Committee on Wireless Broadcasting presented its final report. In that report, and in the debates that followed, it is possible to discern two approaches to radio, one advocating entertainment and the other education. In the report it was argued that cultural progress is more important than entertainment, but Walsh maintained that 'the people want amusement'.[23] In reality these two functions were blurred and both were employed to disseminate Irish culture. Programmes in Irish, however, tended to fall primarily into the educational category.

The main focus of debate over the coming months centred on whether or not an independent company should run Irish broadcasting for profit. During a Dáil debate of the Final Report of the Special Committee on Wireless Broadcasting, Michael Heffernan (Parliamentary Secretary to the Minister for Posts and Telegraphs) argued that he was 'not aware that the supplying of amusements to the public has ever been successfully carried on as a State-controlled business' and went on to claim that 'one of the greatest curses in rural life is the useless way in which people spend their spare time' and that 'it would be a great thing if they could have the advantage of the entertainments placed at their disposal by wireless'.[24]

Conor Flogan took the opposite position, arguing that he was

> mainly interested in this matter from one angle, that of the Irish language, Irish literature, Irish culture and Irish music. I think you can find a very good reason for putting under the control of some national body, such as a State Department, the entire control of everything that appertains to the revival of Irish culture, and everything that is proper

23 Dáil Éireann Parliamentary Debates, 3 April 1924, vol. 6, col. 2879– subsequently cited as 'DD 6' etc.   **24** Ibid., cols 2862–3; also cf. R. Pine, op. cit.

and distinctive in the life of the nation. First of all, it can be used as a medium for cultivating and popularising the study of the Irish language.[25]

He went on to claim that private bodies would not help to cultivate Irish distinctiveness:

> If we let control of this popular and extensive means of cultivating our national distinctiveness pass from our hands into private institutions, we will find that these private institutions will be more interested in producing dividends than in doing any good for the life of the nation.[26]

Many of those who advocated State control also advanced the position that radio should be an instrument of State policy in, for example, reviving Irish. When broadcasting began in Ireland a few years later it was under State control.

2RN

First to be broadcast was 2RN, which began broadcasting from Dublin at 7.45 p.m. 1 January 1926 and could be received as far away as Tipperary, with the right receiver,[27] but for most radios the range was about twenty-five miles. The opening speech was made by Douglas Hyde (founder of the Gaelic League and, later, President of Ireland), who emphasised the importance of Irish for national identity when he said that 'a nation is made from inside itself, it is made first of all by its language'.[28] John Horgan claims that this speech

> underscored an important theme in the station's early years, which was to become something of a battleground in Irish broadcasting later. This was the extent to which the national broadcasting service should – or could – be used as a key element in the official policy aimed at reviving Irish.[29]

In the Dáil, there were regular (or at least annual) discussions about broadcasting in Irish. The reason for this was that, because broadcasting was under State control, each year the Minister was expected to present a report on broadcasting in order to justify the demand for further funding. Most years the Minister (or, in the case of the following quotation, his Parliamentary

---

25 Ibid., col. 2864. 26 Ibid., col. 2865. 27 Cf. R. Pine, op. cit., p. 41 for a discussion of the receivers used at that time. 28 R. Pine, op. cit., p. 187– where the whole speech is reproduced. 29 J. Horgan, *Irish media: a critical history since 1922* (London: Routledge, 2001), p. 18.

Secretary, Michael Heffernan) would make statements such as the following – 'special prominence is, of course, given in programmes to the Irish language, Irish history, music and all subjects of importance to the development of the national characteristics of our people'.[30] Similarly, a few years later, Gerald Boland[31] said that 'special attention is being given to the Irish part of the programme with a view to the extension of the use of the Irish language in programmes generally'.[32]

In the latter quotation we find evidence of an interesting policy, which continued all the way into the television era. The policy is one of diffusing Irish into all aspects of the schedule, including programmes in English. The premise is that by including *cúpla focail* (a few words) in many programmes the audience would be exposed to Irish. It was hoped that this would make Irish a natural part of everyday life. What it did achieve was to reinforce the symbolic position of Irish. People heard and learned a few basic phrases in Irish from the radio. This was similar to the symbolic use of Irish in signs, in official titles and names and at official ceremonies.

Although there were few programmes in Irish on 2RN, much discussion focused on cooperation between the Departments of Posts and Telegraphs and Education to produce lessons in Irish for radio. By and large there were three perspectives on teaching Irish by radio evident in Dáil Debates. Taking one debate in the Dáil on 16 May 1930[33] as an example, none of the speakers objected to the use of radio to promote Irish, but rather to the method of 'teaching' Irish to listeners. Representing the first perspective, Robert Briscoe was critical of the approach taken to the teaching of Irish on the radio and wondered 'if the Department of Education really think that a person listening through headphones or valve sets to the Irish language being read is going, in that way, to obtain an elementary knowledge of Irish'. Séan Goulding, on the contrary, argued 'when I did get Dublin[34] I found the Irish language lessons particularly well done', but that 'Deputy Briscoe reminds me that perhaps I appreciate them because I happen to be a speaker of the language'. Professor W.E. Thrift, representing the final perspective, argued that radio was primarily for entertainment and that lessons should be consigned to a time when they would not interfere with entertainment. He said that

> There is a great deal to be done yet in testing the educational value of broadcasting. Personally I believe it is of great value if done properly, but I think it will have to be done at special times if you are to get value

30 DD 23, 10 May 1928, cols 1285–6.   **31** Gerald Boland was Minister for Posts and Telegraphs, 1933–7. **32** DD 48, 27 June 1933, col. 1379. **33** DD 34, 16 May 1930, cols 2093–101. **34** By 'Dublin' Goulding meant the radio channel 2RN, which was broadcast from Dublin.

out of the educational parts of the programme. You will only succeed in spoiling both parts if you try to mix them up. If you were to get the view of probably 90 per cent of those who listen-in to broadcasting I believe they would tell you that you are making a mistake in forcing Irish on them in the midst of their entertainment. No doubt there are a few enthusiasts like Deputy Goulding who can profit by it. My belief is that they are very few, and if you want to give your instruction in languages I think it should be done at special times when those who want to learn the languages can pay attention to them and get real instruction without interfering with the entertainment that you are trying to give to the far greater proportion of those who pay licence fees.

In general, much of the discussion in the Dáil about broadcasting in Irish on 2RN dealt with how best to employ radio in the interests of the 'restoration policy'. There seemed to be no disagreement with that policy or with the use of radio to promote Irish. The commonly accepted view of radio at the time was that it should be employed 'to help the cultivation of Irish distinctiveness'.[35] This reflected the nation-building ideology of the time.

Although the few programmes in Irish on 2RN reflected the restoration policy, there was a desire there to provide a service for Irish speakers in the interests of the preservation policy. Before the end of the first year of 2RN there was discussion in the Dáil of a separate radio channel for the Gaeltacht. The Postmaster-General explained to the Dáil on 30 November 1926 that a second channel was being built in Cork as a step toward a national station[36] and that there would be a third channel for the Gaeltacht. The high-power station, once built, would broadcast the same programmes as the Dublin and Cork channels to save money by not having more than one programme broadcast at one time. He went on to argue that 'we must exclude from consideration the one in the Gaeltacht', meaning that the Gaeltacht channel would broadcast different programmes.[37] The Gaeltacht channel did not materialise for almost another half a century.

One could speculate that the main obstacle then, and in the decades since, was financial. 2RN itself was controlled by the State and, as such, its expenditure was controlled by the Department of Finance. It was difficult enough to find funding for 2RN, but it would have been even more difficult to overcome the objections to funding a 'minority channel'. An example of that kind of opposition is to be found in a statement by Conor Hogan during the debate of the 1926 Wireless Telegraphy Bill in the Dáil on 7 December 1926. He said:

---

35 Conor Hogan, DD 6, 3 April 1924, col. 2865. **36** Transmitters were not strong enough at that point to have a single national channel. **37** DD 17, 30 November 1926, pp. 356–7.

The Minister for Posts and Telegraphs stated that he was going to erect a wireless station for the Gaeltacht. I confess that I have the feeling that if the Government could give bread to the people there it would be better than giving them a wireless station. We have no information; no figures have been put before us as to what the charge will be on the taxpayer. I do not think it is right that, at present, any money, even one penny, should be expended in respect of this service, which places an additional burden on the taxpayer.[38]

Financial considerations came into play regularly in delaying improvements in broadcasting in Irish. It was argued regularly since the 1920s that it is difficult to justify increased expenditure for programmes that would serve only a fraction of the population. Nonetheless the argument for increased programming in Irish has been made regularly since then. One key example comes from a meeting of the Broadcasting Advisory Committee in 1931, where one member advocated increased programming in Irish; another argued that there must be a relationship between the extent to which Irish is used on radio and the proportion of Irish-speaking listeners; and the representative of the Gaelic League threatened to resign.[39] It was also argued regularly since the 1920s that it was difficult to find sufficient talented Irish speakers to provide increased broadcasting in Irish. Therefore, many of the programmes in Irish were in the form of lessons or the symbolic use of a few words.

Radio Éireann, national identity and Irish
In relation to national broadcasting it appeared that it was not possible to reach the whole country from Dublin or even from the middle of the country in 1927. The Minister for Posts and Telegraphs (previously known as the Postmaster-General) told the Dáil on 30 November 1926 that a high-power station could only reach a radius of 80–100 miles. Broadcasting from the middle of the country would not supply an acceptable quality to the main population centre of Dublin.[40] The Government decided to provide several low-power channels. As it turned out only one other channel was built – in Cork. Cork's '6CK' was officially opened on 26 April 1927. Some of the programmes were produced in Cork, but most were relayed via telephone lines from 2RN. On 30 September 1930 Cork stopped producing its own programmes altogether.

The national station using a more powerful transmitter, which had been discussed during the second half of the 1920s, was eventually established in

38 DD 17, 7 December 1926, col. 485.   **39** Department of Posts and Telegraphs, National Archives file 119/55/2, 27 January 1931.   **40** DD 17, 30 November 1926, col. 356.

the early 1930s.[41] The first broadcasting from this station was earlier than planned in order to broadcast the Eucharistic Congress held in Dublin in June 1932.

This was no coincidence. Another central element of national identity was the establishment of what Liam O'Dowd has called a 'Catholic corporatist order'.[42] The Irish language was not the only element incorporated into national identity. Catholicism also played a central role. Within the national identity of the time (as mentioned above) was an emphasis on a distinction between Irish people, in general, and others, specifically the English. Among the elements of this identity were: speaking a different language (Irish), having different religious beliefs and practices (Catholicism), playing different sports (hurling, Gaelic football etc.) and even having a different socio-economic structure built around a rural agricultural (rather than urban) society. These elements had emerged in the previous century with Catholic Emancipation (1829), the Gaelic League (1893) supporting the Irish language, and the Gaelic Athletic Association (1884) promoting Irish sports. National identity was reflected in broadcasting, through the inclusion of religious, sporting and Irish-language programmes on radio.

A preoccupation with the presentation and representation of Irish 'national distinctiveness' on radio continued with the advent of the national radio station. The concern was to use radio both to build a nation by making Irish people Irish and to represent this nation abroad. In a report requested by Éamon de Valera, the President of the Executive Council,[43] from the Catholic Truth Society of Ireland, F. O'Reilly criticised the national radio station for the impression of Ireland it gives 'outsiders'.[44] Similarly, in a memo to the Government, the Department of Posts and Telegraphs argued that radio programmes should be a 'national pride'.[45] In the Dáil, Tomás Ó Deirg made a related statement:

> Somebody said that European culture was decaying and dying. It was pointed out that even if it were, it still exudes a rather fragrant odour which has a distinct appeal for those who believe in European traditions and European civilisation. If these go, there is no doubt that the world will be the poorer. I think the radio can play a part, and the Irish nation has a special part to play which the radio can be utilised to express and spread in the world abroad in that connection.[46]

---

41 Initially it was referred to as Radio Áth Luain (Athlone Radio). **42** L. O'Dowd, op. cit., p. 33. **43** Later termed Taoiseach and equivalent to Prime Minister in the Government of the United Kingdom. **44** Department of the Taoiseach, National Archives file S3532, 7 March 1935 – subsequently cited as 'DT S3532' etc. or 'DT NA' etc. in the case of more recently categorised files. **45** Ibid., 25 February 1942. **46** DD 121, 25 May 1950, col. 658.

Statements were made annually by the Minister and others to the effect that further money was necessary to improve programmes in Irish or merely that the need for programmes in Irish is constantly borne in mind. The most extreme position was presented in a memo from Conradh na Gaeilge (the Gaelic League) to the Taoiseach (de Valera), in 1939, in which they argued that the amount of programmes in Irish and in English should be equal and that from that benchmark the amount of programmes in Irish should increase until all the programmes on Radio Éireann would be in Irish.[47] Only about 5% of broadcasting time was in Irish at that time (see Table 2.1 for programmes in Irish on Radio Éireann in 1935). A few weeks later the Taoiseach's secretary forwarded the memo to the Department of Posts and Telegraphs. In its response, Posts and Telegraphs claimed that it would not be possible to increase programmes in Irish to 50% of the total and claimed that 'the result, therefore, of any arbitrary attempt to substitute Irish for English programmes on an extensive scale at the present stage might well be that increased numbers of listeners would turn to foreign stations for their broadcast programmes'.[48] It went on to explain that the policy was to increase the amount of programmes in Irish gradually as material became available and to foster material where it is found.

Table 2.1: Irish language programmes on Radio Éireann, 14–20 October 1935[49]

Monday		
Tuesday		
Wednesday	Amhráin [*Songs*]	19.30–19.45
	A Talk in Irish	20.15–20.30
Thursday	Cú Uladh [*Hound of Ulster*]	19.00–19.15
	An Comhar Dramaíochta	
	[*The Drama Partnership*]	20.00–20.30
Friday		
Saturday	An Ceathrar Ceoil	17.30–18.00
Sunday		
TOTAL		105 mins
Percentage of total broadcasting time		4.2

Similarly, in the Dáil, many of the Deputies argued that Radio Éireann should be employed in the interests of the restoration policy. Con Lehane argued that

47 DT S11197A, 22 March 1939. **48** Ibid., 26 April 1939. **49** This table is based on research by the author of radio schedules for October 1935.

> All Parties in this House, or sections of all Parties in this house I should say, pay lip service to the ideal of reviving the Irish language as the spoken language of the country. In Radio Éireann is the ideal vehicle and method of doing it.[50]

In the same debate Éamon Ó Ciosáin maintained that broadcasting is an important resource for reviving Irish. Such statements were made regularly during the period of the 1930s–1950s.

Learning Irish on Radio Éireann

This emphasis on promoting Irish through Radio Éireann was manifest in different types of programmes, such as programmes for beginners, formal lessons, talks about the importance of Irish etc. In 1944, in a memo from Radio Éireann, Séamus Ó Braonáin outlined its programmes for beginners. There were programmes in Irish for beginners at six o'clock in the evening or soon after, everyday except Sunday. The programmes consisted of a talk, songs, music or proverbs on weekdays, mainly for children, and on Saturday evening there was a drama and a programme called *Is Your Irish Rusty?* It was hoped that a book would be produced to accompany this series of lessons.[51] In the Dáil, Patrick J. Little[52] described these lessons saying that 'recently, we have introduced an item the title of which is: "Is your Irish Rusty?" A story is told in English and then in simple Irish by a native speaker, and in that way we are trying to help the language'.[53] This was the first time, according to Little, that Radio Éireann broadcast 'formal lessons'. In the following year he stated

> As regards the Irish language, our policy prior to last year had been to put before listeners programmes in Irish as interesting and as well produced as the programmes in English – but not to broadcast formal lessons. For listeners whose Irish was not fluent, special features, including short stories in simple Irish, were provided, and a weekly programme entitled 'Is Your Irish Rusty?' continues to cater for this class. It consists of the slow reading and translation of passages from short stories and sketches from a set book, an explanation being given of difficult words and phrases.[54]

It is interesting to note the prior policy of presenting listeners with interesting programmes in Irish rather than formal lessons. The policy had been

---

50 DD 117, 12 July 1949, col. 607. **51** DT S13756A, 26 November 1944. **52** Patrick J. Little was Minister for Posts and Telegraphs, 1943–8. **53** DD 91, 25 April 1944, col. 1438. **54** DD 97, 17 May 1945, cols 607–8.

part of the State's effort to 'restore' Irish, and the new lessons reflected these efforts more closely. The prior policy, of avoiding formal lessons, appears, however, to have been a manifestation of an effort on the part of Radio Éireann of avoiding 'ramming the language down people's throats'.

As well as *Is Your Irish Rusty?*, there was a series called *Listen and Learn* which began in 1945. Little explained the context in which this programme emerged:

> During last year much thought was given to the question of making the utmost possible use of radio in the drive for the revival of Irish. Representatives of most of the bodies directly concerned with the movement had frequent consultations with the Director and staff of Radio Éireann and, after full discussion by the Broadcasting Advisory Committee, it was decided to broadcast a series of direct lessons for beginners or for those with little knowledge of Irish. The teaching of a language by radio is, of course, no easy task and in preparation for this particular series, the Broadcasting Advisory Committee and the Department of Education collaborated with the station in determining the form of the instruction. The lessons called 'Listen and Learn' began on Friday, 2nd March, 1945, and have been an outstanding success from the outset. We have evidence that they are being listened to with close attention all over the country by all classes of people and are, indeed, competing with 'Question Time' for the position of the most popular programme from Radio Éireann. I am confident that the lessons will greatly assist many people to learn Irish who, for one reason or another, had not had an opportunity of doing so and were reluctant to attend formal classes. I might repeat, however, that the teaching or the learning of a language over the radio is a most difficult task and suggest that, where classes are available, listeners should supplement the broadcast lessons by attending them.[55]

In the following year Little announced in the Dáil that *Listen and Learn* was 'being followed closely by a large body of listeners', some of whom were from Britain and even some from France. He went on to say that nearly 30,000 copies of the text of the first series and 11,000 copies of the text of the second series had been sold. A recording of the Irish text was also made available by the company His Master's Voice.[56] In 1947, as well as repeating both the elementary and advanced series of *Listen and Learn* Radio Éireann broadcast a series called *Conus Adéarfa* (How would you say)[57] 'to assist accomplished speakers and advanced students to express various ideas in the neatest Irish'[58]

---

55 Ibid., col. 608.   56 DD 100, 30 April 1946, cols 2154–5.   57 Author's translations are provided throughout.   58 Little, DD 105, 23 April 1947, col. 1298.

Listen and Learn competed successfully with programmes in English which, one would expect, have a much larger potential audience. This was not an exception; as shall be seen in the discussion of later decades, there have been a number of programmes in Irish which have been successful in becoming some of the most 'popular' programmes on radio or television.

Collaboration between Radio Éireann and the Department of Education continued with efforts to provide schools programmes in Irish on radio. The following year (1948), the former Minister for Posts and Telegraphs Patrick Little (now in opposition) said that he was

> glad that the Minister has decided to bring the advisory committee into activity again and I hope he will pursue the line we followed of getting Irish taught in the schools over the radio. I do not know how far he has been able to carry out successful negotiations with the Department of Education, but the ideas we had then were that absolutely first-class teachers in Irish would give lessons over the radio to all the schools which took advantage of the radio.[59]

There were discussions in the Dáil about the various methods of teaching Irish using radio. Tomás Ó Deirg argued, in a vein similar to the policy that had existed prior to the introduction of formal lessons in the mid-1940s, that the mere existence of programmes in Irish encourages the public to speak Irish. He said:

> Má chíonn na daoine go bhfuil suim ag lucht an radio, ag na hAirí agus ag lucht an Rialtais sa Ghaeilge, is dóigh liom go mbeidh suim ag an bpobal inti dá réir, agus má fheiceann siad nach bhfuil an Ghaeilge ar an radio ach sa dára háit i gcónaí, ní féidir leis an bpobal bheith muiníneach go bhfuil an Rialtas agus an tAire i ndáirire faoin Ghaeilge a chur chun chinn.[60]

> (If the people see that those in radio, the Minister and the Government have an interest in Irish, I believe that the public, therefore, will have an interest in it, and if they see that Irish on the radio is in second place always, the public cannot be confident that the Government and the Minister are serious about promoting Irish).[61]

During this whole period of the early 1940s, and until the advent of television in the early 1960s, there appears to have been a range and an amount of programmes broadcast in Irish that had not been achieved up to that point (see Tables 2.1, 2.2 and 2.3) and was not even approximated again until the advent of TnaG in recent years. Gorham gave a description of the variety of

59 DD 112, 20 July 1948, col. 833. **60** DD 17, 8 July 1949, 528–9. **61** Ibid.

programmes broadcast during the Second World War years including Irish-language programmes.[62] Music was central – according to Cathcart music programmes accounted for 80% of the total in the 1920s, and although this had decreased to 67% of the total in the 1930s, music continued to be fundamental to Radio Éireann's schedule.[63] News was the other important programme from the beginning, but there were also sports and school programmes. The most popular programme was *Question Time* at the weekend and its partner-programme, *Information Please*, in the mid-week. The poet Austin Clarke ran a poetry competition; there was also a ballad series, and plays were broadcast regularly. On Sunday nights there were charity appeals and most Sundays there was Mass. Some other programmes in English were *Scrapbook for Women, Radio Digest* and *Round the Fire*. Nearly all these programmes had their counterpart in Irish e.g. *Nuacht* (news) and *Tréimhseachán Teann* (current affairs) as well as 'talks, discussions, poetry readings and plays',[64] children's programmes and Irish-language learners' programmes *Is Your Irish Rusty?* and *Listen and Learn*.

As well as attempting to teach people Irish, Radio Éireann used a few other methods to promote Irish. One was to encourage its staff to use a few words of Irish in many programmes in English. Gerald Boland (Minister for Posts and Telegraphs) explained to the Dáil in 1933 that 'special attention is being given to the Irish part of the programme with a view to the extension of the use of the Irish language in the programmes generally'. He went on to explain that they were using a second method to promote Irish by broadcasting talks in English about the restoration effort.[65] Little outlined a similar situation a decade later stating that 'many special talks in Irish and English are broadcast by leaders of the language movement, and short pieces from the writings or speeches of great national leaders on the importance of the language are broadcast at frequent intervals'[66] and in 1953 Erskine Childers[67] explained that 'talks in Irish are now given before broadcasts of big matches'.[68] There were also suggestions from Conradh na Gaeilge that advertisements should be broadcast to promote the speaking of Irish. On 12 March 1953 a delegation from Conradh na Gaeilge had met de Valera (the Taoiseach), who apparently had promised that Radio Éireann would enthuse the public in the support of revival efforts; subsequently, on 29 May 1953 they sent a letter to the Government in which they mentioned this. The letter was sent to the Department of Posts and Telegraphs and a response returned from the 'Gaelic Sub-Committee of the Broadcasting Advisory Committee' that they were reluctant to consider the proposal as they were preparing a full report at present.[69] Similarly on 23 January 1958 a delegation from Conradh na Gaeilge met de Valera (still the Taoiseach) and followed up with a letter to him on 27

62 M. Corham, op. cit., pp. 136–40. **63** R. Cathcart, op. cit., p. 47. **64** M. Gorham, op. cit., p. 139. **65** DD 48, 27 June 1933, cols 1379–80. **66** DD 93, 25 April 1944, cols 1405–6. **67** Erskine Childers was Minister for Posts and Telegraphs, 1951–4 and 1966–9. **68** DD 142, 10 November 1953, col. 1761. **69** DT S14847 and S13756A, January–May 1953.

March 1958 in which they stated that they were aware that the Government was unwilling to take large steps in relation to Irish or to spend much money, but that people should be encouraged to use more Irish and that Radio Éireann could do this. The letter was forwarded to the Department of Posts and Telegraphs and a response came on 8 August 1958 to the effect that people already knew that they could use Irish, but that they would be happy to broadcast such advertisments.[70] The main assumption was that after a few decades of restoration efforts in the education system many Irish people could speak Irish to a certain extent and should be encouraged to use the Irish they have.

Table 2.2: Irish language programmes on Radio Éireann, 12–18 November 1945[71]

Monday	Do'n Aos Óg [*For the Young*]	18.00–18.20
	Na Lóistéirí [*The Lodgers*]	19.30–20.00
	Nuacht [*News*]	22.00–22.10
Tuesday	Do'n Aos Óg	18.00–18.20
	Listen and Learn	21.30–22.30
	Nuacht	22.00–22.10
Wednesday	Do'n Aos Óg	18.00–18.20
	Leabhra Chonnacht [*Books of Chonnacht*]	21.40–22.30
	Nuacht	22.00–22.10
Thursday	Do'n Aos Óg	18.00–18.20
	Amhráin le hAisteoireacht [*Songs with Acting*]	18.20–19.00
	Leabhra Nua-Fhoilsithe [*Recently Published Books*]	19.00–19.10
	Míosachán nua Gaeilge [*New Irish-language Monthly Magazine*]	19.10–19.15
	Nuacht	22.00–22.10
Friday	Do'n Aos Óg	18.00–18.20
	Tráth le Ceol [*Music Time*]	21.00–21.30
	Listen and Learn	21.30–22.10
	Nuacht	22.00–22.10
Saturday	Do'n Aos Óg	18.00–18.20
	Nuacht	22.00–22.10
Sunday	Tásc is Tuairisc [*Report*]	18.15–18.30
TOTAL		460 mins
Percentage of total broadcasting time		10.6

70 DT S3532D, January–August 1958.   **71** This table is based on research by the author of radio schedules for November 1945. The figures for November were used for 1945 because there were

An Irish-language service on Radio Éireann

The two most important types of programmes on 2RN and Radio Éireann during the period 1920s–50s were music and news. There were music programmes in Irish as well. The popularity of music programmes meant that a much larger audience was exposed to the few words of Irish spoken between the music. These programmes, however, had more akin with the dispersion policy (of a few words of Irish in each programme) and to a large extent was a symbolic use of the language. (See Table 2.2 for an example of the types and amount of programmes in Irish on Radio Éireann in 1945).

The news in Irish was as topical in the debates in the Dáil and elsewhere as were the lessons programmes. There was no news in Irish until the late 1930s. It is interesting to note that the two most important types of programmes in Irish – lessons and news – did not begin until years after the radio station began. In 1935 General Richard Mulcahy said that

> we have the position that while news is broadcast twice a day, and while we make provision that piecework placards and lots of other things must be in Irish and English, no news bulletin is sent out from the Broadcasting Station in Irish. The news bulletin has been criticised here. I do not want to go into that, but we hope it will be improved in future … It does seem an extraordinary thing that in a country which is pursuing the language policy that we are pursuing here in the schools and in legislation, the language does not appear to be fit to report the news.'[72]

In a letter to the Minister for Posts and Telegraphs in 1944 the Director of Radio Éireann explained the history of the news in Irish (*Nuacht*) up to that point. *Nuacht* began as *Scáthán na nGaedheal* (Mirror of the Gaels) in August 1938. It was a ten-minute programme at 9.20 p.m. in which recent events would be presented. During that year 2,990 minutes of *Nuacht* were broadcast, which equates to about ten minutes per day. This was not increased until 1950, when extra money was sought by the Minister, specifically to increase *Nuacht* to fifteen minutes per day. One of the problems with *Nuacht* was that it was not always broadcast at the same time. This has been a recurrent problem with programmes in Irish in general. The same programme would not be fixed at a particular time and many of the programmes were one-offs. The result was that there was a lack of predictability and it was difficult to build up a regular audience. *Nuacht* was occasionally switched between 9 and 10 p.m. This unpredictability was a problem associated with programmes in

broadcasts in October from the principal Irish-language festival. Although most of these broadcasts had replaced other Irish-language broadcasts, the festival had, nonetheless, increased the figures by half an hour. **72** DD 56, 15 May 1935, col. 1027.

Irish over the decades on radio and later on television. Steps were taken, occasionally, to fix the time. In 1944 *Nuacht* was fixed to 10 p.m. This did not satisfy everyone, and a number of deputies[73] continued to complain about the timing of *Nuacht*. In 1949 Gearóid Mac Pharthaláin argued that it is not a good idea for the *News* to follow *Nuacht*. He proposed that the *News* be broadcast up to an hour before *Nuacht* and that *Nuacht* could include any additional news that came in after *News* was broadcast.'[74] Conchubair Ó Liatháin made the same argument the following year[75] and similar arguments were made up until the 1980s. Presumably the expectation was that a large audience would tune in to *Nuacht* to get an update. In a similar vein P.D. Lehane made a statement which provides an insight into life at the time and into the importance placed on this minor issue in the Oireachtas.[76] He claimed that

> When we were discussing this Estimate last year, suggestions were made from all sides of the House from Fianna Fáil, from Clann na Poblachta and from myself – that the time the news is read is wrong. The principal news of the night in Irish is read at five minutes to ten. The principal news of the night in English is read at 10.10 p.m. These are extraordinary hours to broadcast the news service. I think Deputy Bartley suggested last year that the news in Irish should be read after the news in English and that the news in Irish should not be a re-hash of the 6 o'clock news. Nothing, so far, has been done in that respect. I suggest that the news in English should be read at 10 o'clock at night and that the news in Irish should be read at 10.15, or vice versa. The present position of the five minutes to ten and the ten minutes past ten news is ridiculous. What happens is that most people do not know when it is five to ten. They know when it is 10 o'clock because they hear some bells ringing round about them. I think some reasonably specific time should be agreed upon for these particular news items.[77]

Another criticism of *Nuacht* which was addressed in 1940 was the provision of *Nuacht* on Sunday as well as the other six days of the week.[78] In that year Patrick Little (the Minister for Posts and Telegraphs) explained the various improvements with respect to Irish on radio. As well as fixing the time for *Nuacht* and adding an additional bulletin on Sunday, Irish was used increasingly in other programmes and there were plays, discussions and native Irish speakers were 'engaged as far as possible'.[79] *Nuacht* on Sunday did

---

73 Members of the Dáil – lower house of parliament.   **74** DD 117, 17 July 1949, col. 623.   **75** DD 121, 25 May 1950, col. 628.   **76** National parliament.   **77** DD 121, 25 May 1950, cols 653–4.   **78** DT S13756A, 28 September 1944.   **79** DD 79, 1 May 1940, cols 2116–17.

not survive. By the mid-1940s there was no *Nuacht* on Sunday, and in 1950 Gearóid Mac Pharthaláin asked 'Tuige a mbíonn oíche an Domhnaigh fágtha amach, i dtaobh nuacht a thabhairt amach i nGaeilge?' ('Why is Sunday night left out, with respect to broadcasting news in Irish?') and continued by arguing that Sunday was the most important day for radio. Bernard Butler agreed, claiming that 'speakers who live on islands, and in backward places, especially, should have their news on Sunday nights presented to them in Irish'.[80] This issue continued to be raised over the following years until in 1954 the Minister for Posts and Telegraphs (Michael Keyes)[81] announced that *Nuacht* was being broadcast on Sundays.[82] It was almost thirty years, from the beginning of radio in Ireland, before news was available in Irish seven days a week.

The time of the broadcast was not the only issue of concern, John Brennan was unhappy with the content of *Nuacht*, arguing that

> What we get is something that I am afraid may be instrumental in killing the Irish language, because it is a rehash of the news of the week in Irish. Do Deputies or anybody outside want to hear the week's news in English, or in any other language, or even of the previous day's news? They do not, particularly in these times when events move so quickly. It is the last word to expect people to listen to such news in the Irish language. I do not know that anyone would do that except enthusiasts.[83]

Several other deputies were unhappy with the dialect and the elocution of *Nuacht* readers. In 1935 General Mulcahy was highly critical, arguing that

> Such broadcasts as are given in the Irish language are to the extent of 90 or 95 per cent nothing but an advertisement that the Irish language as a medium of expression or as a musical language should be scrapped, because the material dealt with in the broadcasts in Irish is hardly worth listening to, and the type of broadcast – the diction, the phrase-ology and the swing of the language – does not represent the living speech that people in the country recognise.[84]

There were many similar complaints over the years and the Minister attempted, as far as possible, to employ native speakers. By the early 1940s there was a newsreader representing each of the three main dialects.[85] Each

---

80 DD 121, 25 May 1950, cols 669–707.   **81** Michael Keyes was Minister for Posts and Telegraphs 1954–7.   **82** DD 146, 23 June 1954, col. 424.   **83** DD 62, 4 June 1941, col. 1502.   **84** DD 56, 15 May 1935, cols 1027–8.   **85** The three main dialects come from the provinces of Ulster, Connaught and Munster.

newsreader had a week each, so that each dialect was represented a week at a time. This did not resolve the issue, as the complaints that came were that their voices were not distinct enough and they did not know how to 'put their voices over the air'. In 1945 the Taoiseach (de Valera) sent a letter to the Department of Posts and Telegraphs in which he complained that the system of having three separate news readers was unacceptable because each newsreader invented new terminology without reference to the others resulting in a lack of consistency. De Valera suggested that one newsreader be employed, who could read the news in Irish and English. This newsreader should have no dialect, or a dialect to which English speakers would like to listen.[86] This episode is amusing. The solution to the problem appeared to be the imposition of a standard of spoken Irish. While this was discussed occasionally, the complaints from some deputies were satisfied when each dialect was represented. The request from the Taoiseach gives an insight into the role of the news. For Irish speakers the news in Irish was a news service in their own language; however, for the Taoiseach, and for many deputies, the news service in Irish was another opportunity to promote Irish (and therefore national identity). There was no RP (Received Pronunciation) and there was no agreement about a standard for spoken Irish, but de Valera's request appears to suggest that the English RP be imposed on Irish so that by making spoken Irish closer to spoken English it would make it easier to understand for listeners who speak English for the most part. It seems paradoxical that de Valera undermined his own version of Irishness in order to promote Irish and Irishness.

The point was made regularly that *Nuacht* was not intelligible for those who could not speak Irish fluently. Some deputies requested that the newsreaders speak slowly and clearly. Others argued, however, that *Nuacht* could be used as a lesson for those with little Irish. For example, Seán Ó Tiomáin argued that

> Níl aon ghné de Radio Éireann is mó a gcuirim spéis ann ná an nuacht sa Ghaeilge. Chun teanga agus saíocht a leathadh, ní dóigh liom go bhfuil áis ann is éifeachtaí ná an craolachán, agus is cóir lán-úsáid a dhéanamh de chuige sin. Do dhaoine a bhfuil roinnt Gaeilge acu, agus do dhaoine a bhfoil meirg ar an eolas a bhí acu uirthi tráth, measaim nach bhfuil aon cheacht Ghaeilge is fearr ná an nuacht sa Ghaeilge.[87]

> (There is no aspect of Radio Éireann in which I have more interest than the news in Irish. There is no resource more effective than broadcasting for spreading the language and culture, and it should be fully

86 DT S13756A, 20 October 1945.   **87** DD 117, 12 July 1949, col. 617.

utilised to that end. No Irish lesson is better than the news in Irish for people who have some Irish, and for people whose knowledge of it has become rusty).

This perspective was taken further when it was suggested to Radio Éireann that it should explain difficult words at the beginning of *Nuacht*. The Director of Radio Éireann, in a letter to his Minister in 1944, said that he opposed the idea of *Nuacht* or other programmes being like a lesson.[88]

Obstacles to Radio Éireann's programmes in Irish
Maurice Gorham argued that 'the Irish side of the programmes suffered from two lasting shortages – of material and of reaction from the audience' during the radio era.[89] This has been a continuing problem for broadcasts in the Irish language during its years from 2RN in 1926 to TnaG in the twenty-first century. As I have argued, the programmes broadcast during the radio period up to (and to a lesser degree beyond) the emergence of television were a reflection of the national identity of the time, attempting to mould, rather than attract, the audience. The promotion of Irish was a central prop in this objective. There were structural obstacles, however, to the achievement of this aspiration. These obstacles are primarily the result of the small number of Irish speakers and the disadvantaged position of native speakers in the Gaeltacht. The continued failure of the restoration policy meant that these structural obstacles remained and the position of programmes in Irish changed little over the decades. These obstacles can be summarised in two categories – staff and audience.

In relation to staff, the Minister (Patrick Little) explained that

> The general policy is, as far as possible, to get the most competent Irish speakers but sometimes it is difficult to combine other qualifications with that qualification. You may have people who are particularly good at music, for instance, but whose knowledge of Irish may not be up to the standard. Sometimes, knowledge of Irish has to be subordinated to technical qualifications but I can assure the House that, wherever possible, we pay due attention to the importance of a knowledge of the Irish language.[90]

It was not only Irish-speaking technicians that were hard to find, but also writers, actors and producers. Radio Éireann had a very limited pool from which to find qualified and competent Irish speakers. In the early 1940s the

88 DT S13756A, 28 September 1944. 89 M. Gorham, op. cit, p. 139. 90 DD 79, 1 May 1940, cols 2128–9.

Taoiseach (de Valera) requested that Radio Éireann desist from employing 'well-paid' teachers and civil servants. The response from the Department of Posts and Telegraphs was that they had no choice; if they were debarred from employing teachers and civil servants there were very few others they could employ. Many deputies expected that all new posts in Radio Éireann would be filled by Irish speakers; even Gorham was criticised for his lack of Irish when he was appointed Director of Radio Éireann in the early 1950s. Oliver Flanagan went so far as to say, 'Might I ask whether it is due to the fact that Radio Éireann is now infested with aliens that the Minister has been prevented from having the news broadcast in Irish on Sunday evenings?'[91] From time to time, however, there were criticisms that Radio Éireann overlooked qualified individuals because of their limited knowledge of Irish. On one such occasion Con Lehane argued that the lack of material in Irish was the result of Radio Éireann's lack of initiative in seeking such material.[92]

In relation to the audience there are two main points – first, Radio Éireann's perspective of the audience and how that influenced programme production, and, second, audience response. It seems that Radio Éireann regarded its audience for programmes in Irish as consisting of two types – the fluent Irish speaker and the potential Irish speaker. The potential Irish speaker was provided with simple programmes in Irish and after 1945 was also provided with formal lessons. The fluent Irish speaker was provided with a range of programmes such as news, talks and drama. This was quite limited: for example, the amount of drama in 1938 averaged one hour per week. Often there were efforts to appropriate programmes which were broadcast for Irish speakers and simplify them sufficiently for learners. There was even a policy not to speak 'in Irish about Irish'. The premise was that by speaking in English about Irish, English speakers might be enthused in support of revival efforts. This policy was occasionally ignored or employed defensively. To give an example of each – in 1951 an item was omitted from the news in English which had been included in *Nuacht*; the item 'was one dealing with an alleged refusal to accept a university diploma issued in English'; the Minister argued that 'the Director of Broadcasting thought it better to give persons interested in matters concerning the Irish language news in Irish rather than in English'.[93] This contradicts the policy of not speaking in Irish about Irish. Yet, in contradiction, in 1965, the Controller of Programmes on Telefís Éireann (Irish television station) refused to cover *Glór na nGael*'s (Voice of the Gael) festival in Irish. He said that 'ós rud é go bhfuil sé leagtha síos mar pholasaí ag an Údarás nach mbeadh cláracha faoi chúrsaí na Gaeilge á gcraoladh tré mheán na Gaeilge, i mBéarla a bheas sé bearthaithe an mír seo a dhéanamh'[94]

91 DD 143, 18 November 1953, col. 266.   **92** DD 117, 12 July 1949, col. 607.   **93** DD 125, 11 April 1951, cols 493–4.   **94** DT NA 96/6/439. 4 June 1965.

('since it is laid down as policy by the Authority that programmes about Irish-language affairs would not be broadcast in Irish, it will be planned to do this segment in English'). This was a belligerent use of a policy for the promotion of Irish in order to refuse a service to fluent Irish speakers.

Listeners' responses to programmes in Irish have tended to be quite limited. On regular occasions there have been very vocal responses, especially criticisms of the lack of programmes in Irish, but there has not been a regular and dependable interaction, however, between programme makers and audiences of programmes in Irish. Listenership surveys were initiated in the 1950s to resolve this problem. This was also a reflection of an ideological shift, as will be argued in the next chapter. As it gradually became clear that the public were not converting to Irish, Radio Éireann slowly shifted to providing programmes for Irish speakers. Nonetheless, the emphasis on propagation remained.

Over the decades the question of how many people were listening to programmes in Irish became more important both because people became more critical of the methods of the restoration policy and because of the slight shift towards providing programmes for Irish speakers. In the mid-1940s *Listen and Learn* was presumed to be one of the most popular programmes on radio because of the response from listeners in the form of letters and purchasing the accompanying text.

In the early 1950s it was decided that surveys should be conducted to ascertain the popularity of programmes. Four surveys were carried out in the early to mid 1950s. These were in March and September 1953, February 1954 and March 1955. There was some controversy about publishing the results. At a Cabinet meeting on 25 September 1953 the Minister for Posts and Telegraphs raised the issue of the results, and especially the problem of the poor showing of Irish – the Cabinet decided not to publish them. The Minister stated in his notes on the survey that 'the only strong adverse vote goes to programmes in Irish' and he went on to say that while this was foreseen 'we will have to have more broadcasts in Irish of live subjects such as sports commentaries. Radio Éireann is considering increasing the proportion of programmes for children in Irish but the quality must be first rate.'[95] Even though the Cabinet decided not to publish the findings, the newspapers and the public in general presumed that the rationale for not publishing the findings was the poor results for programmes in Irish. (See Table 2.3 for an example of the type and amount of programmes in Irish on Radio Éireann in 1955).

95 DT S15580, 25 September 1953.

**Table 2.3: Irish language programmes on Radio Éireann,
10–16 October 1955**[96]

Monday	Clár an Chomhchaidrimh	
	[*Programme of the association*]	08.45–09.00
	Nuacht agus Caint an Luain	
	[*News and Monday's Talk*]	18.01–18.20
	Loch Meilge na Draiochta	
	[*Lake Meilge of Magic*]	19.45–20.00
	Nuacht	22.00–22.15
Tuesday	Nuacht agus Caint Máirte	18.01–18.20
	Blas Aduaidh	
	[*Taste/Accent from the North*]	18.45–19.00
	Nuacht	22.00–22.15
	Amhráin [*Songs*]	23.15–23.30
Wednesday	Scéal an Phíobaire [*The Piper's Story*]	17.45–17.57
	Nuacht agus Caint na Céadaoine	18.01–18.20
	Cérbh é Vittorio Bene	
	[*Who was Vittorio Bene*]	19.30–20.00
	Nuacht	22.00–22.15
Thursday	Cogar a Leanaí [*Whisper Dear Children*]	17.30–17.45
	Nuacht agus Caint na Deardaoine	18.01–18.20
	Nuacht	22.00–22.15
Friday	Amhráin do Pháistí [*Songs for Children*]	17.45–17.57
	Nuacht agus Caint na hAoine	18.01–18.20
	An tEolaire Aoineach	19.00–19.30
	Nuacht	22.00–22.15
	Scéalta Scuir is Codladh Sámh	23.15–23.30
Saturday	Rogha na bPáistí [*Children's Choice*]	17.00–17.30
	Nuacht agus Caint an tSathairn	18.01–18.20
	Aonach na mBailéad [*A Fair of Ballads*]	21.00–21.30
	Bolg an tSoláthair	21.30–22.00
	Nuacht	22.00–22.15
Sunday	Ceolta Tíre [*Country Music*]	13.45–14.00
	Fathach na Fáille	17.00–17.30
	Nuacht Anall, Nuacht Abhus	
	[*News from here, News from there*]	18.01–18.25
TOTAL		537 mins
Percentage of total broadcasting time		8.4

96 This table is based on research by the author of radio schedules for October 1955.

The results show that programmes in Irish had an audience of between 0% and 1%, with *Nuacht* achieving slightly higher listenerships, occasionally reaching up to 7%. The small listenership for programmes in Irish found in the results of these surveys, although expected by the Minister, were a huge blow to programmes in Irish on radio and, soon after that, on television. Broadcasting in Irish reached a zenith by the 1950s; there was a high percentage of programming in Irish, Irish was spoken on many other programmes, a large proportion of Radio Éireann staff were Irish speakers and Irish was the working language for many of them. The one anomaly during this period was that during the height of Irish broadcasting during World War Two many wireless sets were out of commission and parts were not available to repair them. By the 1950s, however, and the lead up to the television era, the perception was that all programmes in Irish had a small audience. The response from then on was not, as the Minister had written, that more and different programmes in Irish be broadcast to attract a larger listenership, but that if programmes have a small audience they deserve small funding.

A separate Irish language radio station?
While programmes in Irish on Radio Éireann increased in quantity during the 1920s–1950s, there were also positive signs of the possibility of a separate radio channel in Irish for the Gaeltacht. Although the expectations of the Minister, that there would be a Gaeltacht radio channel as well as 2RN and 6CK, were not achieved during the 1920s, there was continued anticipation during the 1930s and 1940s in several quarters that it would be realised.

Gorham states that when T.J. Kiernan was appointed Director of the radio station in 1935 he encouraged the formation of a committee in each county to which he would offer access to the airwaves. The first committee formed was in Galway, where they hoped an Irish-language channel would be established. They soon realised that this would not happen and the committee lapsed.[97] In contradiction to Gorham's claim, the initiative had actually come from Galway, according to a letter from the Director to his Minister in 1935.[98] Representative bodies in Galway were demanding their own channel, complaining that people in Dublin had special access to the station. This was particularly the case with respect to auditioning for radio, as auditionees were not paid expenses. People who lived in Dublin had an advantage because they had lower or no costs. In response Kiernan established a committee in Galway to which he would provide access to the airwaves. The committee soon realised that it would not acquire its own channel and the committee lapsed.

97 M. Gorham, op. cit.   **98** DT S3532, September 1935.

The most favourable prospect of a Gaeltacht radio channel came in the early 1940s when Taoiseach de Valera held a meeting on 21 September 1943 with the Secretary and Assistant Secretary of the Department of Posts and Telegraphs and the Director of Radio Éireann. De Valera suggested to them that they investigate the possibility of establishing a special channel, or special channels, for broadcasting in Irish. The reply came in October in the form of an eighteen-page report from a Departmental Committee dated 8 August 1945 and a cover letter dated 30 October 1945 from the Minister (Little) (see Appendices).

In the report they presented a number of obstacles to a Gaeltacht radio channel. First, they claimed that only 10% of households in the rural parts of the Fíor-Ghaeltacht[99] had radios. De Valera had predicted this and had suggested that Radio Éireann distribute radios free of charge. Second, they continued by claiming that the most popular programmes in the Gaeltacht are the same as the rest of the country i.e. the English language programmes. The damaging critique, however, was that radio destroys the Gaeltacht by spreading English. This was based on two points: that people in the Gaeltacht listened to programmes in English because they were more entertaining, and that, although people in the Gaeltacht would make an effort to follow programmes in English, they would not make any effort if they were having difficulty following a programme in Irish in another dialect. Third, it was difficult to get staff who spoke Irish. The overall argument was that, because of limited resources, providing more programmes in Irish would lead to a decline in quality and turn listeners away, so there would be little point establishing a separate radio channel in Irish. Moreover, distributing radios in the Gaeltacht would spread English.

The fourth main point of criticism dealt with technical matters. The committee argued that a national Irish-language channel would require forty channels and eight new wavelengths. To cover the Gaeltacht alone would require ten new channels (and no new wavelengths). They did mention, however, that a FM channel could be achieved with the addition of only four new channels, but that it would require new receivers. Perhaps by broadcasting on FM the problem of switching to an English-language channel would have been avoided. There were no such channels originating in Ireland at the time and presumably none could be received in the Gaeltacht. Regardless, it should have been possible to distribute radios that were set to the Irish-language channel. The cover letter, however, argued that it would cost too much to distribute FM receivers.

The conclusion that came from this Departmental Committee was that the best way to advance Irish was in a schedule of programmes in Irish and

99 Fíor-Ghaeltacht translates as 'Real Gaeltacht' and is the Gaeltacht communities with the highest percentage of Irish speakers.

English. This argument was a manifestation of the restoration policy in which the focus is on promoting Irish rather than on providing Irish speakers with a service in Irish. Had there been the will at this point there would have been a way to provide an attractive radio service in Irish. John Horgan argues that the failure to establish a separate Irish-language radio channel in the 1940s was ideological: he claims that

> The maintenance of intensive language instruction in the schools allowed the perpetuation of the notion that the entire population was, at least potentially, Irish-speaking, and to allow or encourage the establishment of a separate Irish-language station would have amounted to a damaging admission that this was not the case.[100]

This fallacy was dispelled with the arrival of listenership surveys in the 1950s and television ratings in the 1960s.

From the mid-1940s to the 1950s there was an emphasis on attempting to integrate the Gaeltacht into the Irish-language schedule on Radio Éireann by sending recording vans to the Gaeltacht and purchasing superior recording equipment, on occasion, for this purpose. The increase in broadcasts of material from the Gaelt~cht resulted in continuing criticism that the dialects were difficult to understand and the voices indistinct. One deputy even went so far as to claim that 'it does not do the Irish revival any good to hear the awful attempts at what is supposed to be traditional singing. Sometimes it seems as if they are trying to imitate bagpipes and sing through their noses'.[101]

Irish speakers had waited from the mid-1920s to the mid-1940s for a radio channel in Irish and this report postponed the channel again. It would be another quarter of a century before the channel finally began broadcasting.

100 J. Horgan, op. cit, p. 69.   **101** DD 176, 22 July 1959, cols 1666–7.

CHAPTER 3

Changing times: the position of Irish on the new Radio Telefís Éireann

By the mid-1950s the situation of the Irish economy was a matter of grave concern and embarassment. Emigration and unemployment were at a height and the economy was stagnant. There were questions in certain quarters about the viability of an independent Irish State. More particularly, the national identity, and its associated vision, that had been promoted by the State during the previous few decades, came into question. During the late 1950s changes were being made. The Government looked into industrialisation (e.g. *The White Paper on Economic Expansion*, 1958), which would result in a shift away from the protectionist rural agricultural socio-economic structure to a more market-driven economy, a more 'modern' society. Liam O'Dowd believes that this was part of an ideological offensive that was launched by certain academics, economists, civil servants and politicians during this period and has persisted in the decades since.[1] This offensive was against the economic model in particular, but was a more general assault on the earlier aspirations for the nation. While the national identity of the first few decades after independence had been supported by traditionalist intellectuals, the identity that emerged in the 1950s was rational and attempted to break away from the earlier version of national identity. This new ideology attempted to place market forces ahead of identity and emphasise the rational modern individual rather than the importance of national identity in building and holding together the young nation.

The shift from one ideology to another was manifested in the clash of ideas and the coming to power of proponents of the new ideology. The conflict, in essence, was between two national identities – one was the nation-building, traditional, conservative, social identity, the other was the market-building, modern, liberal, individualistic identity. The earlier ideology is characterised by distinctiveness; broadcasting was utilised in the promotion of this distinctiveness in the effort to construct a national narrative. The other

---

1 L. O'Dowd, op. cit., p. 33.

ideology is characterised by convergence; all western European societies converge as the market begins to dominate – identity begins to lose centrality. The convergence ideology means that although the various nations differ in terms of identity, this difference loses significance as all countries become ideologically the same market-driven. Broadcasting reflected this shift as it gradually came under the control of market forces (rather than purely financial restrictions).

Economics is at the heart of the new ideology of convergence. On the European scale this was reflected in efforts to converge economically before embarking on cultural or even political issues.[2] In Ireland this was reflected in the closing economic gap between north and south and cross-border cooperation.[3]

By the 1960s there was a clear opposition between the earlier national identity and the emerging emphasis on market forces. In this context the Irish language was being de-emphasised to the status of individual choice. To deal with this ideological shift Irish-language groups began to emphasise minority rights. This appeared more acceptable within the new ideology. These Irish-language groups began to demand broadcasts in the Irish language on the basis of minority rights. Nonetheless, the earlier national identity endured in opposition to this new emphasis on individualism and the market, and continued to support Irish and broadcasting in Irish, but there was some expectation from then on that it would satisfy market forces.

It was in this context that Irish television emerged. A number of civil servants began to attend international conferences on television broadcasting, there were debates in the Oireachtas about the structure of the new television service, a Broadcasting Bill was passed and Irish television began broadcasting in the early 1960s.

THE NEW NATIONAL IDENTITY

In the first few decades after independence it was imperative for the fledgling state to justify its existence. The promotion of a homogeneous national identity facilitated feelings of identification with the new State (for most of the population). In the 1950s this homogeneous national identity came into question. This was in the context of Europe emerging from the ruins of the Second World War – a context in which nationalism was held to be one of the

---

2 For example, the Coal and Steel and Atomic Energy pacts between France, Germany and Italy in the 1950s, the European *Economic* Community, European *Monetary* Union.   3 Ibid.

causes of that war. From this point onward economics was emphasised in Europe, and nationalism and national identity were de-emphasised. During the 1950s a new generation of economists, academics, politicians and civil servants adopted this new ideology and began to question both Irish economic policies and the homogeneous national identity promoted by the State.

The shift in identity was a gradual process. Elements of the new ideology had been present in the 1920s–50s, but it was not coherent. De Valera's Fianna Fáil party, which had been in government since 1932, was defeated in the 1948 election and the first coalition government was established by John A. Costello. This was not the beginning of the shift – the coalition, according to Horgan,

> was determined not to allow itself to be outflanked on a number of issues which its predecessors had made peculiarly their own, notably those of Partition and the Irish language. It moved, for example, to increase the time allocation on the radio station for the daily broadcast of news in Irish.[4]

De Valera's party came back into power again in 1951 and it is his retirement from the position of Taoiseach in 1959 which is often seen to be the turning point from that older generation to a younger generation with new ideas. Although 1959 was indeed a turning point, the new ideology had begun to emerge in the years before that.

The new ideology that was emerging at this time in Europe was based on notions of citizenship. Citizenship is one method of including individuals in a society. The individual fulfils certain criteria, defined by the state, in order to become a citizen. This is quite different from inclusion based on national identity in which the individual must have the 'correct' set of characteristics that make up that particular identity. The citizenship model of inclusion is less exclusive. Individuals from different ethnic groups, who speak different languages and practise different religions, can become citizens as long as they fulfil basic criteria, such as being born in the country or living there for a certain length of time. Within this model much of the substance of national identity is considered a matter of personal choice based on citizenship rights. The shift in national identity in Ireland was not completely toward this model, but was an attempt to draw on this emerging ideology to argue that Irish citizens should have more choice. This freedom of choice would involve opening up the economy and deconstructing the exclusive homogeneity of national identity.

4 J. Horgan, op. cit., p. 69.

From the 1950s onward, within the emerging ideology, there were efforts to de-emphasise national identity and emphasise the 'modernisation' of the economy. Insofar as this was an attempt to modernise the Irish economy and Irish society, this was a 'modern', as well as a new, ideology. The de-emphasis of national identity involved the argument that many of the elements of national identity should be a matter of personal choice – individual Irish citizens should have the right to choose to speak Irish, but the policy of compulsory Irish in the education system and the promotion of Irish on radio came into question during this period. The Irish language, although an important aspect of Irish society, it was argued, should not be imposed on people.

Critiques of Irish language policy
It was from this point onward that politicians, civil servants and broadcasters no longer presumed that increases and improvements in broadcasting in Irish were expected. Ironically, by the 1940s and 1950s broadcasting in Irish had reached an acceptable minimum in terms of the number of programmes and the standard of those programmes. Up to that point most comments about the service in Irish tended to be critical of its failure to promote Irish. During the 1940s and 1950s deputies in the Dáil praised the service, and the Department of Posts and Telegraphs received little criticism.

During this era, however, criticism began of the Irish-language policy of 'forcing' Irish on radio listeners. In 1949 Captain Peadar Cowan argued in the Dáil that

> When, in company, we have some of these cultural items on the radio, we always hear somebody saying: 'For God's sake turn it off'. That is what happens and those people know that. Nevertheless, they come here and tell us to use the radio for the purpose of strengthening the Irish language, to use the radio for the purpose of making the people speak Irish, to use the radio for the purpose of inculcating a taste for classical music. There is no sense in that approach to the radio because, although you may put these things on the radio, you cannot make the people listen to them.[5]

Similarly, but a decade later, Gerald L'Estrange argued that 'you can sit back and dispense national ideas as much as you like but nobody will be listening except the converted'.[6]

5 DD 117, 12 July 1949, col. 611.   6 Seanad Éireann Parliamentary Debates, 21 January 1960, vol. 52, col. 173– subsequently cited as 'SD 52' etc.

These were initial indications of an emerging ideology in which the promotion of the Irish language was no longer a necessary aspect of Irish political life. In the Dáil, Oliver Flanagan argued that some deputies had gained electoral support by courting the Irish language and Irishness more generally. He claimed that

> There may be a great number of patriotic citizens who are reaping a fairly good reward, directly or indirectly, through the medium of the Irish language.
>
> *Mr Loaghman*: That is a very low suggestion.
>
> *An Leas-Cheann Comhairle*: Order!
>
> *Mr O.J. Flanagan*: There are a number of members in the House who are here because of the stand they take and the way they play up to a certain element in order to obtain the support of those who are believers in the Irish language.[7]

This reflects the conception of ideology. Ideology is a nexus of ideas and behaviour that intersect with positions of power. The Irish language and national identity were ideological because there was an intersection between Irishness and power. The Irish language was ideological to the extent claimed by Flanagan above, insofar as speaking Irish was an important symbol for Irish leaders during the war of independence and in the decades after. In the Seanad,[8] Tomás Ó Maoláin pointed out that the Irish people 'have voted for candidates of political Parties in the forefront of whose programmes has been, by one means or another, the restoring and reviving of the Irish language'.[9] On the other hand, Pádraig Ó Fachma reflected a shift in ideology when he claimed that

> Dúirt Teachta amháin go raibh Teachtaí ar an taobh seo ag cuidiú le labhairt na Gaeilge le vótaí a fhláil. Cé mhéid vótaí a gheothadh duine ar an tsiocair amháin go raibh sé ar thaobh na Gaeilge? Tá sé fíor afach, fo [sic] bhfuil Teachtaí sa Teach seo ag labhairt in éadan na Gaeilge, cionn is go síleann síad go bhfaighidh síad vótaí ó dhaoine atá in éadan athbheochan na Gaeilge.[10]

> (One Deputy said that Deputies on this side were assisting the speaking of Irish to get votes. How many votes would a person get for the sole motive that he was on the side of the Irish language. It is true

---

7 DD 180, 16 March 1960, col. 579.   **8** The upper house of parliament. It translates as 'Senate'.
9 SD 60, 17 February 1966, cols 1502–3.   **10** DD 180, 16 March 1960, col. 584.

however, that there are Deputies in this House speaking against the Irish language, because they think they will get votes from people who are against the revival of Irish).

The debate on the policy of using broadcasting to promote Irish intensi-fied during the 1960s and brought out a number of other arguments which represented a continuing ideological shift. Jack McQuillan argued that

> We should have many discussions on those matters with people whose views differ from ours but who are still Irish and who we hope, in the not too distant future, will come much closer to us on an economic and political basis. I think the economic basis will be closer than the politi-cal basis. I am referring to the different views which are held by a large section of Irishmen on the Irish language and its actual place in the Ireland of the future. There is a small group here who like to dictate policy on the language and who think they will be allowed to make the policy for the entire country. That cannot be tolerated and those of us who have views on that should express them.[11]

The basis of the critique of Irish on television was that the State was being dictated to by a minority in whose interest it was to revive Irish, and that the State was imposing Irish on everyone. In defense of this policy others argued that this minority was not acting in its own interests, but in the interest of the majority and in pursuit of State policy. It is interesting that there was no such critique in the Dáil during the 1920s and 1930s and it only began to emerge from the late 1940s at a time when broadcasting in Irish was beginning to achieve an acceptable minimum. The argument that was emerging at that time, and has never gained full credence, was that the Irish language was a minority issue and that Irish speakers should not be given any special consid-eration, but should be treated equally with all other minorities.

THE EMERGENCE OF TELEVISION IN IRELAND

During the 1950s there was some discussion in the Dáil and in the Department of Posts and Telegraphs both of beginning television broadcast-ing in Ireland and of giving Radio Éireann and the future Telefís Éireann some independence from the State. The autonomy of Radio Éireann raised some apprehension in the Department of Posts and Telegraphs, particularly

11 SD 60, 16 February 1966, col. 1442.

as the Department of Finance wanted broadcasting to be self-supporting. The Department of Posts and Telegraphs sent two memos to Government in 1952 arguing that broadcasting could not be self-supporting. In these memos it emphasised the importance of educational programmes and the use of broadcasting to transmit official information and to revive Irish. It argued that safeguards should be instituted to ensure that such programmes continued to be broadcast by any autonomous body that might be established.'[12]

Television as a commercial venture

During the 1950s there was a gradual distancing of broadcasting from the State. With that distance came a certain autonomy and a little independence from the promotion of national identity. This autonomy began in November 1952 when Erskine Childers appointed a council called Comhairle Radio Éireann and was reinforced in 1960 by the Broadcasting Authority Act.

The period of the 1950s onwards was an era of modernisation in Ireland. During the early part of this era plans were progressing to establish television broadcasting. From 1953 onward, Radio Éireann was considering the factors involved in establishing television in Ireland. Erskine Childers had not been enamoured by television, but with the opening of BBC transmitters in Belfast he began to advocate a first-class Irish television channel to preserve national culture.'[13] After a change of government in 1954, Childers was replaced as Minister for Posts and Telegraphs by Michael Keyes, who was rather cool toward the idea of establishing television in Ireland. As with radio in the 1920s, there was talk of television being a commercial venture. On 6 November 1957 the Minister for Posts and Telegraphs (by that stage it was Neil T. Blaney)[14] declared that Ireland would have television and that it would be 'largely commercial in character' and that proposals would be considered. Blaney did not remain in this office for long. During that same month, at a Fianna Fáil Árd Fheis (party congress), he stated that he would not blame anyone for criticising Radio Éireann as it had disimproved in the three years since it was made more independent. The Director of Radio, Maurice Gorham, threatened to resign as a result of this statement. On 4 December 1957 the Taoiseach moved Blaney to another department, claiming it had nothing to do with the earlier incident.

One of the proposals to run television as a commercial venture was made by Gael-Linn (an Irish-language organisation) – this was the first proposal for an Irish-language television channel. Although its submission was supported by the American Broadcasting Company it was not successful. Gael-Linn's bid and its filming work was appreciated by many. A few years later, in 1960,

12 DT S3532B, 15 and 31 May 1952. **13** DD 142, 10 November 1953, cols 1771–2. **14** Neil T. Blaney was Minister for Posts and Telegraphs, 1957–61.

during the Broadcasting Authority Bill debate in the Seanad a number of Senators requested that Gael-Linn be given responsibility for broadcasting in Irish on the forthcoming television station.[15] This suggestion was not adopted.

On 7 August 1959, however, the Minister for Posts and Telegraphs (Michael Hilliard)[16] announced that television (and radio) would be operated by a semi-state board (the RTÉ Authority) partly funded by licence fees. The Taoiseach, Seán Lemass, had advocated a commercial television station, but he admitted, years later, that he was out-voted at Cabinet.[17] While the new service was not to be a commercial venture, it was clear that a national broadcasting service based totally on licence fees would be too expensive, therefore some advertising was allowed. The legislation necessary to establish the Authority was passed on 6 April 1960.

It was not surprising that a commercial element was attached to the new Authority given the emphasis on economics in the emerging ideology. Even this commercial aspect was moulded to the policy of promoting Irish. It was stated in the Broadcasting Authority Bill that preferential rates be given to Irish companies that use Irish in their advertisements. This was also a source of great debate in the Oireachtas on three fronts: those who disagreed with such preferential rates, those who argued that it would not further the revival of Irish and those who wanted these rates offered to all companies and not restricted to the advantage of Irish companies.

Among those who disagreed with setting such preferential rates in legislation was Edward McGuire, who argued that such power 'should be given to the [RTÉ] Authority' and that 'it should be exercised on their own judgment and not only with the idea of fostering Irish or our national aims'. Tomás Ó Maoláin argued that 'a couple of words of Irish at the beginning or the end or stuck in in the middle … may secure them whatever concession is available, it certainly is of no great advantage to the Irish language or to the engendering of interest in it'. Professor Michael Hayes asked

Does that include foreign advertisers?

Mr Hilliard: No, only Irish firms.

Professor Hayes: Only Irish firms? Then you will preclude non-Irish firms from using the Irish language.[18]

---

15 SD 52, 20 January–10 February 1960, cols 29–562.   16 Michael Hilliard was Minister for Posts and Telegraphs, 1959–65.   17 Cf. J. Horgan, op. cit., p. 82 for an explanation of how this came to light.   18 SD 52, 20 January–10 February 1960, cols 54–485.

Dr John O'Donovan commented sarcastically that advertising in Irish disadvantaged companies and that they deserved to be compensated.[19] In the Dáil, Dr Noel Browne claimed that, as far as he could hear, advertisers did not take advantage of this preferential rate on radio.[20]

As well as brief advertising there were sponsored programmes. There was some argument in the Oireachtas that foreign companies would not alter their programmes to suit Ireland and would broadcast material foreign to Irish culture and that even if they used Irish, it would be just a foreign programme in Irish. Of the 59 sponsored programmes in each week on radio in 1960, two were almost completely in Irish, but came from one organisation, and another ten availed of the concession which allows 150 words of advertising instead of 100, if at least fifty words were in Irish.

A few months later, as a result of these debates, the Minister for Posts and Telegraphs Michael Hilliard, in reporting on amendments to the legislation, stated that he 'came to the conclusion also that the preference for the use of the Irish language should be available to any advertiser'.[21] The preferential rates were retained in the Bill and were extended in the Act.

Measuring the audience

Ratings entered broadcasting at this stage, reflecting the new emphasis on market forces. In 1960 a number of Senators and Deputies argued, as had been argued during the 1950s, that viewership research would be required. From this point on broadcasts in Irish faced one major obstacle – an expectation that they would compete with programmes in English, which had a wider audience in Ireland, supported by the might of broadcasting in English across the globe. Irish and broadcasts in Irish, however, did continue, to some extent, to be protected by legislation.

It seemed from the beginning of RTÉ that ratings would be the factor which would determine which programmes should be broadcast. The first Director-General of RTÉ, an American, Edward Roth, was appointed in November 1960, to serve for a period of two years. In mid-November 1960 Roth gave a press conference at which he maintained that viewership figures would determine which programmes should be broadcast. This viewpoint has continued with the use of TAM (Television Audience Measurement) and then the firm of AC Nielsen to quantify viewership and marks a shift away from constructing a nation toward an emphasis on market considerations. Although the earlier ideology continued to be reflected in the types of programmes broadcast on television – e.g. *Beirt Eile* (Another pair), a traditional music and dance programme, the Angelus etc. – the 'new' ideology,

19 Ibid. **20** DD 179, 24 February 1960, col. 785. **21** SD 52, 6 April 1960, col. 1091.

which seemed to favour a market-driven society, was reflected in allowing the market, through ratings, to determine the types of programmes that were broadcast.

Ratings tell a broadcaster that one channel is more popular than another, that certain times of the day are more popular than others, that certain programmes are more popular than others and that popular programmes can increase the ratings for adjacent programmes, i.e. there is a 'piggy-back' audience[22] who watch a few minutes at the end of a programme before the programme they intend watching commences and a 'follow-through audience'[23] who watch programmes after the programme they had 'tuned-in' to watch. The aim of using ratings is not so much providing programmes which are enjoyed by a large number of people, it is more an attempt to provide advertisers with a large number of consumers and consequently maximising profits within the statutory limits on advertising time. This takes the market rather than the viewer (or the State) into consideration. This is a shift of emphasis from goals (constructing a national narrative) to means (revenue); a shift towards 'instrumental rationality'.[24]

For some types of programmes, such as Irish-language programmes, achieving high ratings is difficult, therefore 'the need to win mass audiences marginalized previously revered types of programmes, such as broadcasts in the Irish language'.[25] Within a few years of the beginning of television broadcasting, John Brennan argued that

> It is not always correct to give them what they want. It could be very simple to give them what they want and be guided by TAM rating entirely. In fact, we would have the Late Late Show the whole day, to take the extreme view.[26]

Within the debate about TAM ratings is the tension between the two ideologies. Ratings is a way of measuring individual choice – a central element of the modern ideology. Others continued to argue that ratings disadvantage all minorities.

On RTÉ this was reflected in increased reliance on advertising (in 1963 income from television advertising was higher than income from television licences).[27] During the debates about television, in 1960, Senator Conor

22 T. Quill, 'Television and the Irish language', *Irish Communications Review* 4 (1994), p. 14.   **23** I. Watson, 'The Irish language and television: national identity, preservation, restoration and minority rights', *British Journal of Sociology*, 47:2 (1996), p. 262.   **24** Cf. J. Habermas, *Communication and the evolution of society* (London: Heinemann, 1979) for an interesting discussion of instrumental rationality.   **25** R. Barbrook, 'Broadcasting and national identity in Ireland', *Media, Culture and Society* 14 (1992) pp. 209–10.   **26** SD 60, 17 February 1966, col. 1578.   **27** L. Doolan, J. Dowling and B. Quinn, *Sit down and be counted: the cultural evolution of a television station* (Dublin: Wellington Publishers, 1969), p. 36.

Cruise O'Brien claimed that 'advertising has a definite commercial value in that it makes competition more keen. The more successful products tend to supplant the less successful'.[28] The result, however, is that the majority is catered for to the neglect of minorities. A conflict ensues between the 'will of the majority', measured by ratings and supported by the modern ideology, and 'previously revered types of programmes', supported by the earlier ideology of distinctiveness.

This 'will' is a measurement of ratings or, as Baudrillard argued, 'the masses are no longer a referent because they no longer belong to the order of representation. They don't express themselves, they are still surveyed. They don't reflect upon themselves, they are tested'.[29] Thus the 'will' is measured from the outside. However, Baudrillard went on to argue that 'today it is necessary to produce consumers',[30] demand must be created. Thus the will of the majority is a measure of the demand (for television programmes, consumer items, education, employment etc.) created exogenously by 'producers'.[31] The earlier ideology attempted to restrict choice to the ideological elements of a distinctive Irish culture. The modern ideology provided as much choice as possible, but the result was that there was not enough demand for all the choice and it became necessary to create demand. In both cases manipulation of the 'masses' was involved.

Market-driven television is (superficially) egalitarian because the viewers get what they want; however, the market itself lacks egalitarianism. Fundamentally, the cost of providing Irish-made programmes is far more than that of buying American-made programmes (£200 as opposed to £20 in the 1960s – equivalent to €2000/200 in 2001), because the American market is large enough to provide the finances necessary to produce high quality programmes for the home market and then sell them abroad at a 'competitive' price. (The American programmes broadcast by RTÉ in the early 1960s were from the 'bargain basement' and had been produced as much as a decade before.) Nonetheless, Irish programmes have a lower average hourly budget (which affects quality) than the programmes RTÉ purchases from abroad and, yet, home production costs more than buying programmes from abroad. The viewers get what they want within the limits of a schedule which is restricted by the cost of home production.

Beyond the constraints imposed by the small size of the Irish market and the resulting lack of financial resources, is the neglect of minorities, if programming is determined by ratings. If programmes were broadcast only because of high ratings, programmes such as Irish-language programmes

28 Quoted in ibid., p. 16.   **29** J. Baudrillard, *In the shadow of the silent majorities* (New York: Semiotext(e), 1983), p. 20.   **30** Ibid., p. 2 7.   **31** Cf. J. Habermas, *The structural transformation of the public sphere* (Cambridge: Polity Press, 1989) for a similar argument.

which could not provide the required ratings would not be broadcast. Thoreau argued, in 1849, against the rule of majority:

> After all, the practical reason why, when the power is once in the hands of the people, a majority are permitted, and for a long period continue, to rule, is not because they are most likely to be in the right, nor because it seems fairest to the minority, but because they are physically the strongest. But a government in which the majority rule in all cases cannot be based on justice, even as far as men understand it.[32]

If the majority 'rule in all cases' with respect to the programmes broadcast on RTÉ, minorities, such as Irish speakers, would be neglected. This argument, which regards Irish speakers as a minority, fits the modern ideology. However, Irish-language broadcasting was supported by the State because of its ideological importance, not because of the rights of the minority.

Within a limited budget it is expedient to focus on the types of programmes which cost less per hour, thereby increasing the possible quantity without necessarily jeopardising the quality. Talking heads programmes are far cheaper to produce than drama programmes, thus it is no surprise that the first programmes produced by RTÉ were of this type: *The Late Late Show* (chat show), *Let's Draw* (children's programmes), *Broadsheet* (public affairs), *Beirt Eile* (traditional music and dance), *Pick of the Post* (sports)[33] as well as similar programmes in Irish, such as *Telefís Scoile* (education), *Labhair Geilge Linn* (Irish-language learners' programmes) (see Table 3.1). Limiting the type of Irish-made programmes to talking heads restricts the creativity of Irish broadcasting to this genre and distorts the worldview presented by RTÉ and the television experiences of the viewers. Desmond Fisher, who was Director of Broadcasting Development in RTÉ in the late 1970s, claimed that

> from the outset, Church authorities, particularly on the Roman Catholic side, were dissatisfied with some aspects of the broadcasting treatment of religion. Irish-language enthusiasts were – and are still – bitterly critical of the comparatively low proportion of Irish-language programming in the television schedules. Sporting organisations wanted better coverage of their fixtures.[34]

Sporting organisations initially, however, had feared a drop in attendance if people could see the competitions on television. These three elements

32 H. Thoreau, *Civil disobedience* (London: Penguin Books, 1995), p. 3 – originally published in 1849. **33** L. Doolan et al., op. cit., pp. 25–6. **34** D. Fisher, *Broadcasting in Ireland* (London: Routledge and Kegan Paul, 1978), pp. 29–30.

(religion, sport and language) are central to national distinctiveness (as discussed above). Mary Kelly argues that

> Public service television and radio are constantly negotiating the interface between national commitments, expressed in terms of home productions which would represent and reflect Irish interests, perspectives and values, including the Irish language, and commercial and profit making demands.[35]

Whatever the impact of television on its viewers, this impact is determined by the skewed nature of market forces.

Table 3.1: Irish language programmes, Radio Telefís Éireann, 11–17 October 1965[36]

Monday	Telefís Scoile [*Schools Television*]	14.15–14.45
	Labhair Gaeilge Linn [*Speak Irish with Us*]	18.01–18.15
	Nuacht	22.50–22.55
Tuesday		
Wednesday	Murphy agus a Cháirde [*Murphy and Friends*]	17.30–17.35
	Labhair Gaeilge Linn	18.01–18.15
	Nuacht	23.00–23.05
Thursday	Nuacht	23.00–23.05
Friday	Labhair Gaeilge Linn	18.01–18.15
	Nuacht	23.05–23.10
Saturday	Nuacht	23.30–23.35
Sunday	Seoirse agus Beartlaí [*George and Bartly*]	16.45–17.15
	Ceamara na Cruinne [*Global Camera*]	17.15–17.25
	Amuigh Faoin Spéir [*Out under the Sky*]	17.25–17.50
	Nuacht	23.00–23.05
TOTAL		170 mins
Percentage of total broadcasting time		6.0

Irish-language programmes suffered as a result of the converging, unifying and levelling force of the market, although, in the 1970s, the English-language current affairs programme *Seven Days* was axed due to a libel case, and the only home produced current affairs programme was *Féach* – in Irish – which achieved very high ratings and cost half its equivalent in English,

35 M. Kelly, op. cit., p. 82.   36 This table is based on research by the author of radio schedules for October 1965.

according to Doolan et al.[37] Nonetheless, Doolan, Dowling and Quinn, who worked in RTÉ[38] in its early years, claimed that

> De bharr an leathcheal atá déanta le fada anois ar chláracha Gaeilge is beag fonn atá ar fiúna stiúrthóirí sa stáisiún a bhfuil Gaeilge líofa acu aon bhaint a bheith acu leo. An té a théann i bhfeighil clár Gaeilge tuigeann sé go mbeidh sé taobh le droch-am craolta agus nach mbeidh na háiseanna ná an t-airgead aige a bheadh aige ina mhacsamhail de chlár i mBéarla.[39]

> (Because of the neglect from which Irish-language programmes have suffered for years, Irish-speaking directors in the station do not wish to be associated with them. Whoever is in charge of an Irish-language programme understands that it will be broadcast at an unfavourable time and that the facilities and finances available to a comparable English language programme will not be made available to it.)

Ratings have caused major change in Irish-language broadcasting. Because of the emphasis on viewership and 'an ideology of competitive individualism',[40] programmes with large audiences have become prized, while Irish-language programmes which had previously been revered become not merely marginalised, as Barbrook[41] claimed, but minoritised. The Irish language was becoming a minority issue rather than a national issue. Programmes in Irish were becoming a matter of minority rights rather than a matter of creating a nation.

WHY HAVE IRISH ON TELEVISION?

The low audience for radio and television programmes in Irish during the 1950s and 1960s led some people to question the purpose of broadcasting in Irish. Nonetheless, the Irish language continued to hold an important role, even in broadcasting. This was reflected in the Broadcasting Authority Act (1960), Section 17 of which stated that

> In performing its functions, the Authority shall bear constantly in mind the national aims of restoring the Irish language and preserving and developing the national culture and shall endeavour to promote the attainment of these aims.

37 L. Doolan et al., op. cit., p. 295. **38** Doolan, Dowling and Quinn worked in RTÉ during the 1960s. Their resignation from RTÉ was considered to be almost a revolt, and their book, op. cit., is seminal. **39** Ibid., p. 295. **40** M. Kelly, op. cit., p. 83. **41** R. Barbrook, op. cit., pp. 209–10.

Figure 3.1: The percentage of total broadcasting time on radio (RTÉ) 1935–55 and television (RTÉ) 1965–99 (the second 1999 bar includes TG4 and TV3) given to Irish language programme.[42]

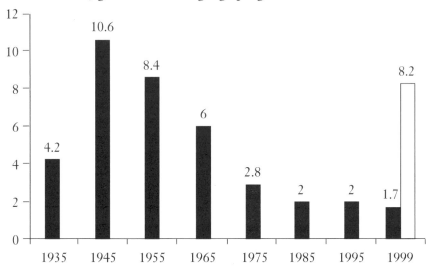

However, according to Gorham, the politicians and 'practical men' did not value Radio Éireann's work for the national culture and would have preferred high listening figures from continuous mass entertainment. Also in relation to the period of the early 1960s, when the Authority took over, Gorham said that 'such guidance as came down from above was to the effect that Radio Éireann programmes ought to be brightened and popularized; Irish language broadcasts and "long-haired" music were understood not to be highly valued'.[43] The Irish language, therefore, seemed to have played a symbolic role on Radio Éireann and it looked as though it would continue in a diminished role on RTÉ (see Figure 3.1).

From the beginning there were problems providing Irish-made programmes, let alone programmes in the Irish language. The Controller of Programmes (Michael Barry) did not begin work until the beginning of September 1961 and broadcasting was to begin in less than four months, at the end of December 1961. The Authority informed the Controller that he was required to provide 42 hours of programmes per week. He began recording programmes all day long, sometimes three or four per day and with a limited budget. Overall, the attitudes of the Director-General, organisational inefficiency (especially employing the Controller of Programmes so late), the limited pool of Irish talent and, moreover, financial constraints, conspired

42 This figure is based on the data in Tables 2.1, 2.2, 2.3, 3.1, 4.1, 4.2 and 5.1. **43** M. Gorham, op. cit., p.315.

against Irish-made television programmes and, moreover, against Irish-language television.

Furthermore, according to Doolan et al. the viewers were provided with a diet of foreign programmes (which they claimed was usually around 60%), mostly American.[44] Although this figure may have been 10% or even 20% lower, it would assuredly affect the worldview presented by RTÉ as the programmes would neither reflect the experiences of Irish people nor the national aims of the State. Roth was asked what kind of programmes he expected to buy and he named a variety of American programmes – *Bugs Bunny, Perry Mason, Father Knows Best, Life of Reilly, Gunsmoke* – and 'asked whether the station would have to follow the policy of the Government in order that the service should have an Irish outlook he said he didn't think so',[45] 'he insisted that in the early stages of Irish television we would have to rely heavily on the purchase of American filmed programmes'.[46] This was mainly because of financial constraints.

Continuing the old policy

The debate about Radio Éireann's role in relation to Irish-language policy continued in the Oireachtas during the first year or two of the 1960s. The debate was similar to that of the previous decades. There was a continuation of the discussion of the timing of the news in Irish, relative to the news in English (this issue re-emerged from time to time until the 1980s). There was also continued criticism of Radio Éireann's work for the language. One deputy even went so far as to claim that listening to Radio Éireann was like a penance:

> Deputy Corish talked about the Irish language and what happens in Radio Éireann. I may not agree with him or he may not agree with what I say, because I would go much further than Deputy Corish. I have listened to Radio Éireann, particularly in the last twelve months, in order that I would be in a position to discuss it from experience. I must confess that to listen to the productions night after night was one of the greatest penances I ever had to impose on myself. I was often tempted to give way to the feeling that takes possession of a person and to put a sod of turf through the radio.
>
> Deputy Corish referred to the question of the Irish language and Radio Éireann. It is beyond contradiction that there are people in Radio Éireann concerned with Irish programmes who have done harm to the Irish language. Once their voices are heard on Radio Éireann

44 L. Doolan et al., op. cit.   **45** Ibid., p. 20.   **46** Ibid., p. 24.

listeners switch to another station. It seems to be the policy of those responsible for programmes in Irish: 'We must give so many hours to the language'. It is like a religion. After that the directors of the programmes, like Pontius Pilate, wash their hands of the whole affair, and we find the same group there week after week. They are not there for the love of the language alone. They are very well paid by the taxpayers for the hours of nonsense they produce in the Irish language.[47]

The situation on Radio Éireann was quite similar during the 1960s to the way it had been during the 1950s. About 10% of broadcasting from Radio Éireann during the 1960s was in Irish. Once Telefís Éireann began broadcasting in 1962, there was hardly a mention of Radio Éireann's work for the language.

Some of the same discussion continued, but in the new, and different, context of television. The discourse on distinctiveness from the earlier ideology is clear in the debates over television. Many Irish households on the east coast and near Northern Ireland could receive television broadcasts from the United Kingdom with the use of an aerial. Erskine Childers said that television should develop and promote Irish culture,[48] and the Television Commission (established by the Minister for Posts and Telegraphs in March 1958) feared that without an Irish television channel Ireland would suffer from cultural osmosis which would result in the loss of cultural distinctiveness.

The criticisms of broadcasting in Irish which had been quite frequent in the 1930s, but had gradually declined during the 1940s and 1950s 'golden era' of broadcasting in Irish, gained frequency again in the 1960s because of the perceived neglect of Irish on television. Radio Éireann, on the other hand, continued to broadcast about the same amount of material in Irish during the 1960s as it had in the previous two decades. In 1964 the Minister for Posts and Telegraphs, Michael Hilliard, claimed that 10% of total time was devoted to Irish speech material.[49]

Telefís Éireann came in for criticism, however, particularly for the limited number of programmes in Irish. In response to such criticism the Minister argued that he was

> satisfied that in the circumstances with which the Authority are confronted, they have been doing the best they possibly can for the Irish language. The time devoted to Irish is two hours in a weekly schedule of forty-two hours. It looks low, of course, and does not show up well

47 John McQuillan, DD 180, 16 March 1960, col. 623. **48** L. Doolan et al., op. cit., p. 7. **49** SD 57, 26 February 1964, col. 559.

the effort in this matter of propagating, to some degree at least, the Irish language.[50]

In 1962 Conradh na Gaeilge claimed that there was only one hour of broadcasting in Irish per week.[51] A few years later the situation had hardly improved and John Geoghegan complained that 'coming from the Fíor-Ghaeltacht, I feel very strongly that 15 minutes, one item a week, is too short a time to give to our native language'.[52]

At the beginning of the previous year the Government had set up an Irish-language advisory committee (Comhlacht Comhairleach na Gaeilge). In April this committee wrote a letter to the Minister for Posts and Telegraphs in which they were very critical of the RTÉ Authority's work in promoting Irish. The Committee protested that

> the extent to which those services have helped to promote the restoration of Irish over the last five years has been extremely disappointing. Furthermore, it appears to us that any little recognition given to Irish on the television service was conceded only after intense effort on the part of the language organisations. We feel that much more should be expected from any service established by the State, and particularly the Broadcasting Authority, the all pervading influence of whose services could virtually decide whether Irish is to be restored or not.[53]

At the beginning of Telefís Éireann's first year of broadcasting there was only one hour of programming in Irish,[54] this increased to two hours a few years later.[55] By the late 1960s programming in Irish had increased to twenty hours per week, but in 1969 there was a reduction of two hours in programmes in Irish and an increase of the same amount in bilingual programmes. The policy at that time was to include as much Irish as possible across a range of programmes. This policy was called the 'diffusion policy' and disparagingly dubbed the 'confusion policy' by a number of RTÉ staff. The objective was to expose as large an audience of non-Irish speakers to a few phrases in Irish and was a continuation of the earlier nation-building policy of attempting to teach the whole population Irish.

Associated with the diffusion or bilingual policy was the policy of not talking about Irish in Irish. This was a continuation of policy from the radio era into the television era. The argument was that any discussion about Irish

50 Ibid., col 560.   **51** DT S11197 D/63, August 1962.   **52** DD 220, 1 February 1966, col. 607.
53 DT NA 96/6/439, 9 April 1965.   **54** Memo from Conradh na Gaeilge: DT S11197 D/63, August 1962.   **55** Hilliard, Minister for Posts and Telegraphs, SD 57, 26 February 1964, col. 560.

should be done in English so that all listeners could be influenced. This was part of the restoration policy, but did not conform to the needs of Irish speakers as manifested in either the preservation policy or the minority rights approach. In 1965 there were protests (mentioned above) from the Irish-language organisation Glór na nGael because Telefís Éireann refused to broadcast highlights of the Glór na nGael Week in Irish.[56] Telefís Éireann said that it would broadcast highlights of the 'week' on the English-language news programme *Newsbeat*. Glór na nGael complained that this policy undermined the service given to Irish speakers.

This policy and the bilingual programmes were a reflection of the restoration efforts associated with the old ideology in which programmes in Irish were aimed at 'converting' the population. The perspective of the new ideology was that Irish-language programming should be aimed at Irish speakers, not to preserve the language, but rather, as a minority right.

Regardless of the emergence of a 'modern' ideology, the former 'nation-building' ideology continued and a tension or a dialectic emerged between the two. As had been, and continued to be, the case with radio, television was used to present the Irish audience with Irish lessons. In 1960 Dr Owen Sheehy Skeffington argued, as if nothing had changed in Irish society, that Irish lessons on television should improve on those formerly broadcast on radio. He claimed that:

> The Authority must be allowed ... to do the job, not perfunctorily but intelligently, as if people wanted to teach Irish and not as if they wanted slabs of it churned out to a non-listening public. I do not think our language-teaching by radio – there have been exceptions; I am not condemning all of it – has been as imaginative as it could be and, consequently, as effective as it could be.[57]

During that same debate Éamon Ó Ciosáin maintained that the bulk of the restoration effort had been imposed on the education system and that television could be of service to the policy of restoration. He said 'is ar ghuaille na múinteóirí a thuit an t-ualach go hiomlán cheanna maidir le cúrsaí na Gaeilge agus tá súil agam anois nuair a bheidh an Teilifís ag obair go bhfaighidh na múinteoirí cabhair uaithi'[58] ('the weight has fallen fully on the teachers' shoulders with respect to Irish-language matters and I hope now that Television will be working that the teachers will receive assistance from it'). Also continuing within the purview of the earlier restoration policy, Pádraig Ó Fachtna made it clear that he felt that broadcasts in Irish were not mainly for Irish speakers

56 DT NA 96/6/439, 4 June 1965.   **57** SD 52, 21 January 1960, col. 162.   **58** SD 52, 20 January 1960, col. 72.

when he claimed that 'the bulk of the programmes must, in the main, be in simple language'.[59] This was partly a criticism by some who felt that Radio Éireann had moved away from teaching Irish and that most of the programmes in Irish on radio could only be understood by fluent Irish speakers.

Although this debate appeared to reflect the earlier ideology, there was a new element emerging from the 'modern' ideology. Irish was not held with the same homage as it had been. Until the 1940s, for some, the aim of the restoration policy also included the objective of gradually increasing the proportion of broadcasts in Irish in direct relation to the increase in the numbers speaking the language. Those who disagreed with this intention did not begin to voice this objection with any frequency until the 1960s. By the 1950s it became apparent that this objective (and many other objectives) of the nation-building ideology was not being achieved.

It could be said that the new element that permeated the restoration objective was realistic insofar as it accepted the failure of the policy up to that point. On the other hand there is a certain paradox in the willingness to use television to teach the population Irish while also being critical of the aim of restoring Irish. Nonetheless, much of the discussion of Irish lessons on television, in the Oireachtas in 1960 (just prior to the beginning of Telefís Éireann), involved a certain dilution of earlier aims. One clear example is Patrick W. Palmer's claim that while television should be used to promote the learning of Irish he hoped 'that amongst the members of the Authority there will be no fanatic who thinks that all programmes should be in Irish. In fact, there should be no kind of fanatic amongst the personnel of that Authority'.[60]

Regardless of Irish lessons and the diffusion policy, by the late 1960s criticism continued of Telefís Éireann's broadcasting in Irish. Before Telefís Éireann began there had been some considerable demands by certain members of the Oireachtas that the Director-General of RTÉ and at least one member and the Chairman of the RTÉ Authority should be Irish speakers. Yet, according to Dónall Ó Móráin (a member of the RTÉ Authority and Gael-Linn), much of the blame for the meagre performance of Telefís Éireann in relation to Irish could be blamed on the members and employees of the Authority. In 1969 he wrote a letter of complaint to the Chairman of the RTÉ Authority, Dr C.S. Andrews. Ó Móráin said that he was unhappy with RTÉ's record of broadcasting in Irish and complained that the Director-General's attitude was 'very disappointing'. He went on to argue that some of the decisions of the Authority, which had been based on statutory duties, had been 'filtered' by RTÉ staff and that some of the staff hired for bilingual programmes were 'virtual monoglots'.

---

59 DD 180, 16 March 1960, col. 590. **60** DD 179, 24 February 1960, col. 767.

Interestingly, Ó Móráin divided the 1960s into five phases in terms of Irish-language programmes:

1 Up to June 1965 there was very little use of Irish on television and there was an actual decrease in the amount of Irish on radio.
2 From June 1965 to February 1966 there was conflict between some newly appointed members of the Authority and the Chairman and Executive. The written policy of the time was constructive, but was not implemented.
3 From February 1966 to June 1966 the Chairman and the Executive fought to prevent the implementation of policy.
4 From June 1966 to April 1968 there was a Chairman with a more favourable attitude towards Irish. The Executive, however, continued to resist.
5 From April 1968 to January 1969 there were senior executives who did not oppose Irish-language policy. Although the Authority, the Chairman and the Executive did not oppose Irish-language policy there was no progress on television and a decrease in the amount of programmes in Irish on radio.[61]

The criticisms of broadcasting in Irish on radio were repeated in the debate about setting up the television station. Members of the Oireachtas and of Irish-language groups warned that the programmes in Irish on television should be better than they were on radio; that programmes in Irish should be of a high quality and not made merely to achieve a high quantity; that those in charge of RTÉ should be Irish speakers; and that Irish speakers on Telefís Éireann should have an acceptable level of fluency. Programmes in Irish on Telefís Éireann during the 1960s, however, were far fewer than those on Radio Éireann during the 1950s, and there were even programmes in which Irish and Irish-language policy were attacked. Critics of Radio Éireann's work for the language shifted from trying to achieve a higher quality and quantity of programmes in Irish before Telefís Éireann began in 1962, to fighting for a minimum quantity of programmes in Irish on Telefís Éireann after 1962.

It appears that from a position of strength in the 1950s Irish-language broadcasting came under attack from supporters of the modern ideology who maintained that broadcasting in Irish did not have popular support and should therefore be considered a minority interest. Even those who continued to argue for improvements in broadcasting in Irish began to include phrases to modify their statements. Some would say something like 'I'm not a fanatic' or 'I disagree with those who would like only Irish on Telefís Éireann' before arguing that Telefís Éireann was not providing the minimum amount of programmes in Irish. These speakers seemed to feel a need to dissociate themselves from some earlier attitude and align themselves with a new 'modern' attitude. This reflects the ideological shift. In relation to broadcasting there was an ideological shift from using broadcasting as a tool of language policy to regarding broadcasting in Irish as a public service.

Attacking the old policy

The poor performance of programmes in Irish on Radio Éireann (according to the listenership surveys of the 1950s) and on Telefís Éireann (according to the TAM ratings) reinforced the view within the emerging ideology that Irish speakers were a minority and the programmes in Irish should be minority-interest programmes. This was part of the critique of the failure of earlier nationalist objectives. There was also a belief that popular opinion was turning against the imposition of Irish on pupils and on viewers. John Benignus O' Quigley argued in the Seanad in the mid-1960s that

> the first thing we must do in this country, in order to secure any kind of advance in the love and learning of Irish, is to get rid of a whole lot of misconceptions in relation to it; to quiet a great number of fears which exist and to eliminate, as far as is possible, a number of the existing prejudices against it.[62]

The new emphasis on ratings prompted some members of the Oireachtas and others to argue that most people disliked programmes in Irish and would change channels or switch off. Based on this belief, they argued, it would be pointless to impose the language on people. For example, Oliver Flanagan argued that 'people do not want to listen to Irish; they are not listening to it and will not listen to it'.[63] For some the answer was to decrease the quantity of Irish on radio and television, for others it was to improve the quality.

There was some disquiet that RTÉ itself was turning against the language. Comhlacht Comhairleach na Gaeilge (a committee set up by the Government) complained that many programmes on Telefís Éireann ridiculed the restoration aims. Similarly, Conradh na Gaeilge protested in letters to the Taoiseach in 1962 and 1963 that Telefís Éireann should not use popular programmes to 'belittle Irish'.[64] A rebuke came from the Department of Posts and Telegraphs; it declared that Conradh na Gaeilge should not contact the Government, but should work through Comhdháil Náisiúnta na Gaeilge (a state-sponsored national Irish-language body), which should contact the RTÉ Authority. It added that it had expected a report from RTÉ

62 SD 60, 16 February 1966, col. 1462.   **63** DD 180, 16 March 1960, col. 579.   **64** DT S11197 D/63, August 1962 and 1 October 1963.

on the current situation of broadcasting in Irish, but that it had not been forthcoming.[65]

The complaints about negative discussion of Irish on television continued through the 1960s. For example, in the Seanad, Dermot Patrick Honan outlined a situation in which he

> was amazed three months ago when viewing a teenage programme to hear one of the panel make a most awful attack on the Irish language in the presence of many young people. I thought, perhaps, his patience had overcome him, but since then I heard the same person in another programme make what I considered to be a most unwarranted statement against the language. I am not a language enthusiast but I am dedicated and feel like everybody would that everything should be done to revive Irish, and I do not see, whatever we talk about minorities, any reason why a person who is known to be actively adverse to the language should be put on a programme in the position of a compère. Let him to get out into the middle of the floor where he will have to take any criticism that comes from there. I would not put any man in the exalted position of being on the panel who was known to take that attitude. He should not succeed in getting back on this panel after what he said on the first occasion.[66]

One programme provoked considerable debate on this issue in the Seanad. A number of Senators had participated in a debate on *The Late Late Show* to mark the publication of the White Paper on Irish in 1965. In the Seanad Garrett FitzGerald (later Taoiseach) claimed that the television debate had been between those who supported the current Irish-language policy and those who did not. He went on to complain that Telefís Éireann was expected to 'balance' the two sides of the argument in favour of current policy. He claimed that all the participants in the television debate were advocates of the Irish language, but that Joe Lynch had joined him in criticising current policy. Senator Thomás Ó Maoláin objected to Lynch's style of debate saying that he had been 'clowning about'. Ó Maoláin and others in the Oireachtas and elsewhere complained that the whole debate had been biased against the language and that it was an attack against the State's Irish-language objectives and the language itself.[67]

Both Fitzgerald and *The Late Late Show* embodied the new ideology. Fitzgerald argued that it was undemocratic for a minority to dictate to the majority. He connected the controversy to Northern Ireland by claiming that

---

65 Ibid., 9 October 1963. **66** SD 60, 17 February 1966, cols 1559–60. **67** Ibid., 16 February 1966.

there were other minorities in Ireland that were ostracised by national policy, which disseminated and protected an exclusive and homogeneous national identity. He linked the controversy to notions of democracy, citizenship and, within that, minority rights. He expressed the main thrust of the new ideology, in which the Irish language, although remaining of symbolic importance, was of minority interest. Many advocates of Irish, who disagreed with the de-emphasisation within the new ideology, were willing to adopt the minority-rights approach to Irish.

The Late Late Show in its early years was new, dynamic and innovative; it was critical of the old ideology. Horgan claims that 'it was also, incrementally, about the development of a new orthodoxy, which challenged the old, Gaelic and somewhat authoritarian one, or at least constructed an alternative lens through which it might be viewed'.[68] Time moved on, however, and *The Late Late Show* and the new ideology became 'traditional' and old fashioned as new developments emerged.

---

68 J. Horgan, op. cit., p. 89.

CHAPTER 4

Separate station: Raidió na Gaeltachta and the early TV campaigns

The late 1960s was a period of mass protests in the western world. It was a period when the philosophy of rights was reflected in the emergence of social movements. Ireland was no exception. There were rights-based protests in the Gaeltacht. By 1970 it was clear that for the first time a separate radio channel in Irish was to be established. However, preceding the establishment of RnaG were protests which continued for about three years. In December 1968 a group, based in Cork, calling itself 'Coiste Práinne na Gaeilge' (The Irish Language Urgency Committee) wrote an open-letter addressed to the Taoiseach in which it stated 'tá ré na rún imithe' ('the era of passing motions has gone') and announced that it was organising a demonstration in Cork on 25 January 1969. It demanded a radio and television channel in Irish for the whole country.[1] RTÉ was considering the issue of a separate Irish-language radio channel during this period and informed the Department of Posts and Telegraphs, orally, that it ruled out the idea because of the economic and technical difficulties involved. RTÉ did state, however, that it had a project in mind to involve the Gaeltacht – it intended sending a mobile studio to the Gaeltacht in the autumn.[2] The momentum was maintained by Conradh na Gaeilge when it sent a letter to the Secretary to the Government, that same month (December 1968), in which it included a motion, passed by its members, requesting the Government to establish an Irish-language radio channel for the Gaeltacht and all Irish-speaking families.[3]

A response to the question of a separate television channel in Irish came from the Department of the Taoiseach in January. It argued that the Commission for the Restoration of Irish did not recommend a separate

---

1 DT NA 96/6/439, 6 December 1968.   2 Ibid., 11 December 1968. This is very similar to the response to de Valera's request in the 1940s for a Gaeltacht radio station – at that time Radio Éireann sent a mobile recording van to the Gaeltacht.   3 Ibid., 30 December 1968.

channel in Irish. It favoured bilingual programmes on RTÉ.[4] This statement characterised the state policy to revive Irish and missed the point being made by the Irish-language organisations. These organisations were arguing that RTÉ was teaching people Irish and not serving Irish speakers. This represented the new ideology. The Irish-language organisations were adopting the minority-rights argument from the new ideology by claiming that they were a minority, but they held on to the old ideology to claim that they were a minority of national importance. They used this argument to demand a better broadcasting service in Irish. The State's primary policy in this respect was to revive Irish and the implementation of this policy in broadcasting did not serve Irish speakers. The Department of the Taoiseach also stated, in its letter, that the arguments made in 1945 were still effective.[5] Presumably it was referring to the report of the Departmental Committee of the Department of Posts and Telegraphs on the feasibility of a Gaeltacht radio channel. The main argument at that time was that radio spreads English and since only 10% of households in the Gaeltacht had a radio it would be necessary to provide them with radios and this would spread English in the Gaeltacht. This argument would not have been relevant for radio by the late 1960s, and if radio was already spreading English in the Gaeltacht, then so would television, eventually.

In February or March 1969 the Government asked RTÉ for a report on the feasibility of a Gaeltacht radio channel.[6] This was based on a request for a report, in the White Paper on Irish which had been published in March 1969. It was at this point that demonstrations began in the Connemara Gaeltacht, which culminated in the establishment of RnaG. On 18 March 1969 demonstrators picketed the RTÉ quizshow *Quicksilver*, protesting at the broadcasting from the Gaeltacht of a programme in English. A few days later some of the demonstrators and others met in a local school and drew up a provisional list of demands for improvements in the Gaeltacht. This list did not include the demand for a radio channel. The group met again a few days later and established Gluaiseacht Cearta Sithialta na Gaeltacht (Gaeltacht Civil Rights Movement) and set out its list of demands, which included a radio channel. According to Niamh Hourigan, 'Des Fennell, a well-known journalist and academic based in Connemara, suggested the inclusion of a demand for a Gaeltacht radio station'.[7] During 1969 Gluaiseacht ar son Cearta Sibhialta na Gaeltachta began demonstrations in Galway, demanding rights for people in the Gaeltacht. This movement reflected the broader

4 Ibid., 16 January 1969. **5** Ibid. **6** It is unclear whether this request was made in February or March. Cf. DT NA 96/6/439 29 April 1960, DT NA 2001/6/98, 11 August 1970 and N. Hourigan, *Comparison of the campaigns for Raidió na Gaeltachta and TnaG* (Maynooth: Department of Sociology, National University of Ireland, Maynooth, 2001), p. 99 for differing accounts. **7** N. Hourigan, op. cit., p. 27.

international civil rights movements and discourse of the time. But it also recognised the Irish language as a minority issue and speakers of that language as a minority group.

In April 1969 the process gained momentum. The Taoiseach, Jack Lynch, who was attending a seminar organised by the Irish Committee of the Munster Branch of Fianna Fáil on 4 April, was approached by a delegation[8] demanding a radio channel in Irish for Munster. A report of the meeting appeared in the Irish-language newspaper *Inniu* in which it was claimed that the Taoiseach had agreed to do his utmost to establish a radio and television channel in Irish as soon as possible and that RTÉ would receive an order from Government.[9] This latter statement caused a minor commotion when the Taoiseach denied that he ever said that RTÉ would receive an order from Government.[10] In mid-April the Gaeltacht Civil Rights group marched in Dublin to highlight its wider demands and also picketed a local river to demand the return of fishing rights to local inhabitants.[11] The pressure was mounting on the Government and on the Minister for the Gaeltacht, who wrote to the Taoiseach complaining that he was still awaiting a report from RTÉ, on the feasibility of a Gaeltacht radio channel, over a year since it had been requested.

In the General Election in June the leader of the Gaeltacht movement, Peadar Mac an Iomaire, stood unsuccessfully for election. His manifesto included a number of demands for the Gaeltacht, but did not include the demand for a radio channel. In the autumn it was clear from a number of articles in *Inniu* that the campaign for a Gaeltacht radio channel would continue (e.g. 19 September and 24 October 1969). The authors of these articles intimated that people in the Gaeltacht might start an illegal radio station. The first article (on 19 September) made the threat more convincing as it was written by the Movement's press officer.

At this point RTÉ sent its response to the request to assess the feasibility of an Irish-language radio channel. It complained that it required an increase in the licence fee, that a separate channel would be too expensive, but that a Gaeltacht channel would be easier to establish than a national channel. It suggested, however, that a segment for the Gaeltacht from 18.45 to 19.45 each evening on the new VHF channel would suffice.[12] This was clearly a half-hearted response – RTÉ had also claimed in the letter that it was awaiting permission to establish a VHF channel and that there were only 50,000 VHF radios in the country. A response came from the Department of the Taoiseach chastising RTÉ for failing to submit a full report.[13]

---

8 N. Hourigan, op. cit., p. 99 claimed that this delegation was from Conradh na Gaeilge. **9** DT NA 96/6/439, 24 April 1969. **10** Ibid., 25 April 1969. **11** N. Hourigan, op. cit., p. 99. **12** DT NA 96/6/439 17 October 1969. **13** Ibid., 23 December 1969.

At the end of the following March the civil-rights group set up its own illegal radio station called Saor Raidió Chonamara (*Free Radio Connemara*) and broadcast on 28–31 March 1970. Although the authorities closed down the station, demands for an Irish-language channel continued. Hourigan argues that the pirate station was successful insofar as it neutralised 'the two major objections to Gaeltacht radio repeatedly articulated by authorities: the cost of the service and the lack of Gaeltacht staff capable of running the station'.[14] In April Coiste Práinne na Gaeilge wrote to the Taoiseach requesting permission to set up a radio channel for the Gaeltacht in Corca Dhuibhne (Co. Kerry)[15] and in May the Connemara group also wrote to him and to the Department of Posts and Telegraphs requesting a licence to broadcast.[16] At the end of May the Minister for Posts and Telegraphs informed the Dáil that he did not intend to give these groups licences. The Minister for the Gaeltacht had already given a commitment to the Seanad in late April that a Gaeltacht radio channel would be established. Hourigan makes an interesting argument that 'the establishment of Raidió na Gaeltachta represented a successful attempt by elites to neutralize Gluaiseacht' rather than deal with the other demands of the group.[17]

In June RTÉ finally delivered its report on the feasibility of a radio channel in Irish. It favoured three small studios in the three main Gaeltachts – in Ceathrú Rua in the Connemara Gaeltacht, in Gaoth Dothair in the Donegal Gaeltacht and in Corca Dhuibhne in the Kerry Gaeltacht. The Minister for the Gaeltacht and for Finance (the same person – George Colley) agreed that the Gaeltacht channel should be set up urgently, but subject to consideration of responsibility.[18] At a Cabinet meeting in October 1970 the Government committed itself to establishing RnaG with the annual running costs coming from the licence fee and capital costs not to be borne by RTÉ. It also agreed that the question of responsibility was still to be determined.[19]

Regardless of these commitments the Connemara group kept up the pressure. In November 1970 it re-established its pirate station to broadcast its own cultural festival called 'Oireachtas na nGael' (Conference of the Gaels). Hourigan reports that activists felt that they got away with these pirate broadcasts without being arrested because of the sympathetic views of the local superintendent Patrick Gallagher.[20] Later that same month the Government announced publically that a radio service was being established for the Gaeltacht and would begin broadcasting at the end of the following year.[21]

The debate about who would be responsible for RnaG continued. Conradh na Gaeilge objected to RTÉ having control because of its poor

14 N. Hourigan, op. cit., p. 33.   **15** DT NA 2001/6/98, 9 April 1970.   **16** Ibid., 12 May 1970.
17 N. Hourigan, op. cit., p. 43.   **18** DT 2001/6/98, 11 August 1970.   **19** Ibid., 9 October 1970.   **20** N. Hourigan, op. cit., p. 34.   **21** DT NA 2001/6/98, 26 November 1970.

record in programmes in Irish.[22] The Minister for the Gaeltacht also expressed this opinion and proposed that a group of seven representatives should control RnaG, but under the legal framework of RTÉ. These would be – the Director-General of RTÉ, the Chairman of the RTÉ Authority, two representatives from the Department of the Gaeltacht and one from each of the three main Gaeltachts. He also argued that RnaG personnel should be paid by RTÉ. If RTÉ would not cooperate, he maintained that legislation should be changed to allow a separate RnaG Authority.[23] The Minister for Posts and Telegraphs agreed in general with this proposal, but stated that the Chairman of the RTÉ Authority should also be the Chairman of Comhairle RnaG (the RnaG Council) and that the head of RnaG would be responsible to the Director-General of RTÉ as well as to the Comhairle. RTÉ would also supply support – technical, accounting, specialised programming, radio library and archives, production outside the Gaeltacht, news material etc.[24] In July the Cabinet agreed with this, so long as the Department of Posts and Telegraphs was represented on the board that was to choose the Head of RnaG.[25] Later that same month the Connemara group nominated Peadar Mac an Iomaire to Comhairle RnaG. The Comhairle was announced in September 1971 and Mac an Iomaire was not appointed. Hourigan argues that this was part of the isolation by the authorities of the Gaeltacht Civil Rights Movement in order to deflect their demands.[26]

During that summer an amusing note came from the Department of Posts and Telegraphs in which a civil servant argued that the new Irish spelling 'raidió' should not be used for Raidió na Gaeltachta. Attached to this note was a memo from Posts and Telegraphs to Finance in October 1958 in which it argued that the modern Irish spelling for words such as 'radio' is longer and would cost more on letterheads and signs. It also argued that they would be put to expense in having to change signs throughout the country. It also argued that 'radio' is an internationally recognised spelling. Based on this 1958 memo, the civil servant argued that the new channel should be called 'Radio na Gaeltachta not 'Raidió na Gaeltachta'.[27]

During this period the redefinition of national identity within the modern ideology was evident in some discussions of RnaG and of the Gaeltacht Civil Rights Movement. Nationalism, and often extreme nationalism, was linked with the Irish language by some people. During the civil-rights movement some people felt it was a wing of the IRA or at least a manifestation of nationalism.[28] On the contrary, many of those involved had a very 'regional' view and

---

22 N. Hourigan, op. cit., p. 100. **23** DT NA 2002/8/156, 25 May 1971. **24** Ibid. **25** Ibid., 6 July 1971. **26** N. Hourigan, op. cit., pp. 43 and 100. **27** DT NA 2002/8/156, 6 July 1971. Interestingly Raidió na Gaeltachta is spelt 'Radio na Gaeltachta' in the publication of the Dáil Debates. **28** Cf. D.R. Browne, 'Radio na Gaeltachta: swan song or preserver', *European Journal of Communications* 7 (1992) 416–17.

argued that the Gaeltacht had been neglected in the pursuit of more general restoration policies regarding the Irish language. In relation to RnaG, the Irish language was again directly linked to nationalism when 'certain Dáil members were opposed to what they saw as ... a divisive service ... divisive because Irish speakers "had a different agenda", allegedly favouring more radical action to reunite Ireland'.[29] RnaG began broadcasting in April 1972 and was nationwide within a few years. Criticisms of RnaG continued from some politicians and RTÉ officials who could not understand Irish well enough and felt if it was in Irish it had something to do with violent nationalism.[30]

RTÉ hired seven people to run RnaG (six teachers and one businessman) and broadcasting began on Easter Sunday, 3 April 1972. The members of the Comhairle were located in the Gaeltacht in the hope that this would reinforce the aim of RnaG – to serve the Gaeltacht. This aim suits a minority rights policy, but at the same time some people in RTÉ and some politicians felt that RnaG should be maintained strictly within the Gaeltacht, thus attempting to restrict the Irish language to the minority, rather than allowing it to be a national issue. 'RnaG staff determined from the outset that the service would not limit itself to mirroring everyday life in the Gaeltacht, although there were RTÉ officials who thought that it should'.[31] This is illustrated by RnaG's attempts to use Irish speakers throughout the world as correspondents and RTÉ's attempts to restrict RnaG's news to what RTÉ supplied.

Although RTÉ officials and certain politicians, according to Browne,[32] seemed to be attempting to limit RnaG to the lifeworld[33] of the Gaeltacht, nonetheless, RnaG has managed to some degree to reflect a more national and international worldview and to show that the Irish language can be used to discuss the modern world. A major criticism has been that RnaG reflects too much of the 'old fashioned' lifeworld which the younger population find irrelevant and unreal for their life. While RnaG is a Gaeltacht channel, the young people in the Gaeltacht, according to one Gaeltacht activist (Donncha Ó hÉalaithe), are as urbane as young people in the rest of Ireland.[34]

Although research is infrequent, RnaG seems to have a regular and substantial listenership. A survey carried out by sociology students from National University of Ireland, Galway in 1979 found that 35% of all Gaeltacht people listened to RnaG 'yesterday';[35] and studies carried out by the MRBI (Market Research Bureau of Ireland) found that of all adult radio listening in the

29 Ibid., pp. 417–18. **30** Ibid., pp. 427. **31** Ibid., pp. 423–4. Cf. also R. Ó Glaisne, *Raidió na Gaeltachta* (Indreabhán: Cló Cois Fharraige, 1982), p. 220. **32** Ibid. **33** Everyday life as experienced by members of society. The original German term is *lebenswelt*. **34** J. Gogan, 'Ar Aghaidh Linn' *Film Ireland* April/May, 1996, p. 16. **35** T. Fahy, 'Listenership up 10 percent', *Irish Broadcasting Review* 8 (1989) 56–7.

Gaeltacht RnaG had 43% in 1988, 32% in 1995 and 41% in 2001. As well as listeners in the Gaeltacht, RnaG has listeners from across the country and, via satellite and the internet, from other countries.

Before, and ever since, it began broadcasting, RnaG was enthusiastically acclaimed in the Dáil and the Seanad. Some argued that it gave people in the Gaeltacht a sense of belonging and an opportunity to talk to one another, others that it fulfilled the State's language policy to some extent. RnaG was discussed as an exciting and innovative 'experiment'. John O'Donoghue went so far as to say that

> Since its formation Radio na Gaeltachta has been a model for every local radio station, its contribution to the people of the Gaeltacht being indeed significant. Indeed the argument could be advanced that the Irish language would be in a poorer state today were it not for their outstanding contribution. It has been a model of consistency, of truth, and continues to render an outstanding service.[36]

In the mid-1970s, however, the Minister for Posts and Telegraphs (Conor Cruise O'Brien)[37] who was regarded by defenders of the old ideology as an antagonist, was accused of attempting to 'kill' RnaG. In the Dáil, Jim Tunney launched a scathing attack on the Minister, accusing him of attempting to relegate RnaG to broadcasts in the morning only and for failing to appoint a new Head of RnaG.[38]

THE MODERN IDEOLOGY IS REDEFINED

The modern ideology that had been developing during the 1950s and 1960s encountered an obstacle to its objective of overcoming conflict over identity. This obstacle was the violence in Northern Ireland from the end of the 1960s onwards. Until that stage advocates of the new ideology were content with emphasising economics and de-emphasising identity. They attempted to relegate identity to the position of individual choice and free will. Since then there has been a systematic removal of compulsory elements of the language policy and a repositioning of Irish as a purely minority issue.

This is reflected in two issues of relevance that were debated in the Oireachtas during the 1970s – the Broadcasting Authority (Amendment) Bill 1975 and the second national television channel. In both cases Cruise O'Brien

36 DD 399, 29 May 1990, col. 692.   37 Conor Cruise O'Brien was Minister for Posts and Telegraphs, 1973–7.   38 DD 294, 17 November 1976, cols 131–2.

was denounced as an enemy of the Irish language. What is interesting in this debate is the manner in which Cruise O'Brien and his supporters exemplified the new ideology and his detractors represented the traditional ideology.

During these debates the redefinition of the 'modern' ideology was evident. The outbreak of the conflict in the North threatened the new ideology in the sense that the old national identity and its associated nationalist discourses might re-emerge. Later in the 1970s and more evidently in the 1980s the economic situation began to worsen. Throughout the 1970s and 1980s problems associated with both the economy and Northern Ireland re-emerged. 'As the Northern conflict has persisted however, the Southern intellectual began to change orientation to national identity. Whereas in the 1960s, questions of national identity and sovereignty were set aside in favour of other national goals, in the 1970s and 80s, there has been a concerted attack on "nationalism".'[39] It is probable that this attack on nationalism has been focused rather generally on the earlier national identity and on all discourses pertaining to it, and may even include the discourse on the Irish language (as is clear from the attacks against RnaG discussed above). The result has been more of an attempt to redefine national identity than a rejection of it.

The Broadcasting Authority (Amendment) Act

O'Dowd's claim that intellectuals launched an attack against nationalism seems to be reflected in the 1976 Amendment of the 1960 Broadcasting Authority Act. In the 1960 Act (quoted above) there is a focus on restoring the language and on the national culture, however, the Broadcasting Authority (Amendment) Act, 1976 Section 13 (a) states that

> The Authority shall: Be responsive to the interests and concerns of the whole community, be mindful of the needs for understanding and peace within the whole island of Ireland, ensure that programmes reflect the varied elements which make up the culture of the people of the whole island of Ireland, and have special regard for the elements which distinguish that culture and in particular the Irish language.

Against the background of the violence in Northern Ireland, which had started approximately seven years earlier, it seems interesting to note that the 1976 Act mentioned 'peace', 'culture' and 'the Irish language' together as if to suggest that there was some link between the Irish language and the conflict in the North. This amendment reflected the political situation in Ireland and as such must be taken in that context. However, as well as the attack

---

39 L. O'Dowd, op. cit., p. 35.

against nationalism implied in this amendment there is also a reflection of the fragmentation of identity ('varied elements which make up the culture') and of the persistence of the Irish language as a marker of distinctiveness ('in particular the Irish language'). Thus, this amendment reflected the dialectical opposition of the two ideologies.

In the Seanad and the Dáil there were a number of individuals who argued against the amendment of Section 17 of the original act. Michael Mullen claimed that the amended section would 'do harm to the language and to Irish culture'.[40] George Edward Russell joined him, arguing that 'it does not fulfil what I would regard as one of the most important functions of the national broadcasting service'.[41] Michael Yeats argued vehemently that the new wording would 'disregard the entire concept of an Irish nation or of Irish nationality' and went on to claim that

> had the marvels of modern science developed sufficiently so that television could have been inaugurated in 1900 this is just about how it would have been in the conditions when we were still part of the United Kingdom of Great Britain and Ireland.[42]

A few months later, at the report stage of the Bill, Seamus Dolan attempted to argue against the wording in a manner that might appeal to Cruise O'Brien. He began with an invocation to the earlier ideology, stating 'Measaim gurb í an Ghaeilge agus labhairt na Gaeilge [atá] bunúsach don náisiúntacht'[43] ('I think that the Irish language and the speaking of Irish are fundamental to nationality') and then went on to argue

> Tuigeann an tAire féin fosta go bhfuil ana-suim ag na daoine sna Sé Chontae – a lán acu – sa Ghaeilge agus cuireann sé áthas orthu an Ghaeilge a chloisteáil. Ní h-iad na daoine ar a dtugtar náisiúnaí orthu atá meas acu ar an Ghaeilge ach na daoine atá dílis do Shasana b'fhéidir. Tá ana-mheas acu ar an Ghaeilge freisin. Tá a fhios agam féin ó scríbhinní a thagann chugam ón Ulster Folkschool agus daoine mar sin go bhfoil siad ana-bhródúil gur cuid de mhuintir na hÉireann iad.[44]

> (The Minister himself understands also that the people in the Six Counties – a lot of them – are very interested in Irish and they are pleased to hear Irish. It is not the people who are called nationalists who respect Irish but the people who are loyal to England maybe.

---

40 SD 79, 12 March 1975, col. 827.   **41** Ibid., 19 March 1975, col. 887.   **42** SD 80, 16 April 1975, col. 303.   **43** SD 81, 25 June 1975, col. 1407.   **44** Ibid., col. 1408.

They have a lot of respect for Irish also. I know from writings that come to me from the Ulster Folkschool and people like that that they are very proud that they are part of the people of Ireland).

In arguing this point Dolan was attempting to counter the logic of the ideology underlying Cruise O'Brien's text – the Irish language was an element of Irish nationalism, Irish nationalism is a factor in the violent conflict in Northern Ireland, therefore the Irish language is an agent of violence or a cause of conflict. The other Senators and Deputies argued that the amendment of Section 17 by Section 13 was a 'national sabotage', but Dolan attempted to break the logic of the new ideology and appeal to this ideology on its own terrain.

During the 1950s and 1960s advocates of the 'modern' ideology had emphasised economic modernisation and disregarded national identity and nationalism. They appear to have been following the rationalism of European unification in which it was hoped that economic unification could overcome the violent nationalism that had divided Europe previously. By the early 1970s, however, it was clear that this approach was not working in Northern Ireland. It was at this time that promoters of the 'modern' ideology, such as Cruise O'Brien, began actively to de-emphasise what they regarded to be the props of nationalism and to emphasise democracy and minority rights – with Northern Protestants in mind.

As well as juxtaposing 'peace' and 'Irish' in Section 13, this perspective is evident in Cruise O'Brien's response to Michael Yeats:

> Senator Yeats' amendment puts more emphasis on the concept of Irish identity and less emphasis on the cultural variety that exists in Ireland. I consider the latter emphasis the more realistic because when we use phrases like 'essentially Irish', and 'Irish identity', we are in some danger of setting up a graven image which we would be hard put to define. For example, Senator Yeats said, and I would agree with him, that what he has in mind is the whole people of Ireland, including, of course, 1 million Ulster Protestants whose allegiance and outlook are in significant ways different from the remaining inhabitants of the island.[45]

Yeats was critical of the Minister's tenacity in persisting with his original formulation of Section 13 even though he had accepted amendments to other sections of the Bill. He argued that Cruise O'Brien connected the Irish language and Irishness with extreme nationalism insofar as

45 SD 81, 6 June 1975, col. 1035.

he drags illegal armies and Republicans of all kinds into a matter which I would have thought had very little relation to them. Apparently, the very concept that we should aim to provide a broadcasting service that is essentially Irish in content and character to the Minister smacks of sinister Republican bands. I did not envisage sinister Republican bands as making their way through the wording of this amendment. It seemed to me to be an essentially cultural matter. Since the Minister apparently associates this with some form of extreme Republicanism.[46]

Similarly, Jim Tunney claimed that 'when one speaks of the Gaelic tradition in the Minister's presence it appears to disturb him slightly'.[47] In contradiction Cruise O'Brien argued that there are different types of Irishness and that he did 'not regard the test of a person's Irishness as the degree of his anti-Britishness'.[48] He explained that he was not against the Irish language, instead he argued that

if we can strip the Irish language, and the culture associated with it of the accretions of exclusivism and even the humbug which have surrounded them, and if we can see them as a significant part of our heritage, but neither its totality nor its sacred, dominating element, then spontaneous interest in and love for these things can reassert themselves. Certainly that concept is reflected in the relevant part of the Bill before the House.[49]

Table 4.1: Irish language programmes on Radio Telefís Éireann, 13–19 October 1975[50]

Monday	Nuacht	19.00–21.00
	Feach [Current Affairs]	21.30–21.50
Tuesday	Nuacht	19.50–21.00
Wednesday	Nuacht	19.50–21.00
Thursday	Nuacht	19.50–21.00
Friday	An Choill Mhór [*The Big Woods*]	16.55–17.00
	Nuacht	19.50–21.00
Saturday	An Saol Beo [*The Living Life*]	18.30–19.00
	Nuacht	19.50–21.00
Sunday	Nuacht	19.50–21.00
TOTAL		115 mins
Percentage of total broadcasting time		2.8

46 Ibid., 25 June 1975, col. 1415.   **47** DD 294, 17 November 1976, col. 130.   **48** SD 81, 6 June 1975, col. 856.   **49** DD 285, 28 October 1975, col. 409.   **50** This table is based on research by the author of television schedules for October 1975.

In the Seanad, arguing in support of the Minister, Brendan Halligan claimed that 'the national aim of restoring the Irish language was assumed into the general duty without much analysis or debate. The Minister's reformulation of the general duty of RTÉ corresponds more closely with the reality'.[51]

The dialectic between the two ideologies reflected a conflict between a nation-building exclusive identity formed in opposition to Britishness and its antithesis which was attempting to be inclusive by de-emphasising this sense of identity constructed in the earlier ideology and, instead, stressing democratic principles and minority rights.

The second channel debate

The dialectic between the two ideologies continued in the debate over the second national television channel. Again the 'modern' ideology was represented by the Minister for Posts and Telegraphs, Conor Cruise O'Brien, who proposed that the second national channel be used to re-broadcast either BBC Northern Ireland or UTV (Ulster Television). He had two objectives in mind. The first was to satisfy the demands of viewers who could only receive RTÉ. Some people, who could only watch RTÉ and had no viewing-choice, protested that many other people in Ireland could watch British channels. A couple of principles of the 'modern' ideology, such as equality, free choice and the freedom of the market, were at issue here. The second objective Cruise O'Brien had in mind was to make an arrangement with British authorities to broadcast RTÉ in Northern Ireland in exchange for the re-broadcasting of BBC Northern Ireland in the Republic.

In the Seanad in 1975 Mary Robinson (later President of Ireland) outlined the developments in relation to the second channel that had occurred up to that point. She began her account in March 1973 when the first interim report of the Broadcasting Review Committee was presented. She said that the report outlined four possibilities: broadcasting a foreign channel, a second RTÉ channel, an RTÉ monopoly of cable for all the larger cities or RTÉ as at present with private companies to provide foreign channels in larger areas. The Committee concluded in favour of a second channel for RTÉ. A few months later, in May, the Minister spoke in favour of broadcasting a foreign channel. Soon thereafter the Broadcasting Review Committee presented its second interim report, which again recommended that RTÉ broadcast the second channel. RTÉ supported this conclusion. In October the Minister stated that the Government had authorised the provision of a transmitter network and microwave link network which would serve for

---

51 SD 80, 17 April 1975, col. 374.

broadcasting either one Northern Ireland television service or a second RTÉ channel. In December, Irish Actors Equity, the Irish Federation of Musicians and Allied Professions, British Actors Equity, and the British musicians' unions met and issued a statement that 'the proposal to hand over an Irish television station to a foreign broadcasting authority, ... while affecting the volume of employment for Irish performers on television, would also weaken the national cultural identity and reduce RTÉ to an irrelevancy'.[52] In January 1974 Sir John Eden, the British Minister of Posts and Telecommunications, stated that the British Government would not be obliged to broadcast RTÉ in Northern Ireland. In May the RTÉ Authority, realising that the Minister did not seem to be in favour of a second RTÉ channel, put forward an alternative proposal on co-operative broadcasting, co-operative in the sense that RTÉ would select worthwhile programmes from a range of broadcasting services outside the country'.[53]

The debate revolved around Cruise O'Brien's proposal to re-broadcast BBC and opponents who advocated RTÉ-control of a second channel. To a large extent this debate reflected the division in the 'Amendment Debate' between the 'modern' and earlier ideology. Supporters of re-broadcasting BBC argued that it created competition in the television 'market' in the Republic, that it offered viewers choice and that it demonstrated to Northern Protestants that we were not 'inward looking'. Opponents argued that the Government would 'if not entirely kill RTÉ, certainly reduce RTÉ to a tiny minority viewing programme'.[54]

In the Seanad, Austin Deasy defended the Minister's position by arguing that 'the people want the rebroadcasting of this second service from either BBC 1 or ITV in its entirety' and went on to state that 'too much of the programming which has gone on in RTÉ 1 since its inception has been at the behest of minority groups whose influence is far beyond the number of people they represent'. In this context he was referring to Irish speakers, this is clear when he continued by stating that he did 'not believe that people who advocate the putting on of an Irish language programme at peak periods in the evening can honestly be classified as having the general interests of the public at heart'.[55]

The main position in this debate, in relation to the Irish language, was that rebroadcasting BBC would put RTÉ in the position of competing with BBC on its terms, which would result in the gradual disappearance of Irish from television. Similarly, it was argued that a second RTÉ channel could be used to complement what became RTÉ1. The two channels could be used to broadcast both the more popular American and British programmes as well

52 SD 79, 19 March 1975, cols 933–9. **53** Ibid. **54** Senator Robinson, ibid., col. 946. **55** SD 81, 25 June 1975, col. 1371.

as programmes which promoted Irishness. John Kelly argued against the logic of this thesis, stating

> I observe that in my own Dublin suburban constituency, which is exposed to every British channel, there are more Irish speakers, if you do not mind taking that as a convenient criterion, and more Irish enthusiasts than there are, I believe, in some western or southern four-seat or three-seat constituencies. There are more Irish enthusiasts in the postal districts Dublin 6 and Dublin 14, both of which I represent substantial parts of.[56]

This argument missed a few points, however. Viewers in Dublin had the opportunity of watching Irish programmes on RTÉ, but with the introduction of BBC across the country in competition with RTÉ, some argued that the Irish flavour could vanish from RTÉ. The result would have been the elimination of all programmes in Irish from television. A second contradictory point was that there were very few programmes in Irish on RTÉ and many of these programmes were aimed at promoting Irish among learners or among those with little Irish.

Irish on RTÉ appeared to be of symbolic importance to most people, as it was in ceremonial occasions, in streets signs, company names etc. For Irish speakers the symbolism was regarded as a half-hearted gesture. There was a clear tendency amongst Irish speakers, from the period of the Gaeltacht Civil Rights Movement onward, to regard themselves as a minority (albeit symbolically important) with the right to be entertained and informed in Irish by RTÉ. Bilingual programmes and the 'diffusion' policy were of little service to them.

In October 1975 the idea of re-broadcasting BBC was abandoned. The Minister announced that

> Doubts were raised as to what the people, particularly those in single-channel areas, really wanted and in order to resolve this, a survey was sponsored jointly by my Department and RTÉ in order to determine what the public preference is. As Deputies will be aware the results of the survey which was carried out by Irish Marketing Surveys Ltd. were announced recently.
>
> The survey showed a clear preference for RTÉ 2 over BBC 1 (Northern Ireland) in both the single-channel and the multi-channel areas. The percentages were: 62% for RTÉ 2 and 35% for BBC 1 overall.[57]

56 DD 285, 30 October 1975, col. 653.   57 DD 285, 28 October 1975, col. 382.

Cruise O'Brien had already announced in the Dáil that he would abide by the majority decision of the survey.

Irish-language organisations were afraid that programmes in Irish would be banished to RTÉ2. Barbara O'Connor argued that 'with the advent of RTÉ2 it was feared by certain groups that Irish language programmes might be relegated to the less popular second channel'[58] which had been set up to broadcast mainly foreign programmes. She argued that during the years 1979–81 the percentage of programmes in Irish on RTÉ1 (*vis-à-vis* RTÉ2) declined from 89% to 68% and back up to 78%.[59] During the 1980s there was a gradual transfer of Irish-language programmes to RTÉ2/Network2[60] (see Table 4.2). This transfer of Irish-language programmes to what has sometimes been termed 'the less popular channel' has been regarded as causing a decline in the audience of these programmes.

Irish-language organisations, as well as individuals and groups of Irish speakers continued to demand throughout the 1980s that RTÉ increase the amount of programmes in Irish on its two television channels. Gradually, during the decade the emphasis began to shift toward a separate television channel in Irish.

IMPROVEMENTS ON RTÉ OR A SEPARATE STATION IN IRISH

Increased programming on RTÉ

Dissatisfaction amongst Irish speakers with broadcasting in Irish was manifested in demands for an increase in the amount of programmes in Irish on RTÉ as well as demands for a separate channel. The demands for a separate Irish-language television channel were made regularly and range back as far as the late 1950s, when Gael-Linn proposed to establish and operate Ireland's television station. A decade later Doolan, Dowling and Quinn, who had been working in RTÉ, suggested having a Gaeltacht television channel.[61] Another decade later Bord na Gaeilge published a plan for improving the situation of Irish in which it recommended that an Irish-language television service for the Gaeltacht be established.[62] Although there were such infrequent demands for a separate television channel in Irish, many of the regular protests, during the 1970s and even into the 1980s, were focused on increased programming in Irish on RTÉ1 (and later including RTÉ2).

---

58 B. O'Connor, *Irish language media: discussion document* (Dublin: Bord na Gaeilge, 1983), p. 5.
59 Ibid. 60 RTÉ2 came on the air on 2 November 1978 and was relaunched as Network2 a decade later in 1988. 61 L. Doolan et al., op. cit. 62 Bord na Gaeilge, *Action plan for Irish 1983–1986* (Dublin: Bord na Gacilge, 1983), p. 5.

During the 1960s and 1970s most of the energy of protests in relation to broadcasting in Irish went into demanding improvements in the quantity of programmes in Irish on Telefís Éireann. The percentage of programmes in Irish on television was only about 2%, in comparison with almost 10% on radio during the 1940s–60s. The demonstrations during the late 1960s culminated in the establishment of a Gaeltacht radio channel in the early 1970s. This channel had been expected on a number of occasions ranging back to the 1920s.

Although a separate Irish-language television channel was never really seriously expected until the 1970s, Gael-Linn's offer in the 1950s to run Irish television gave brief optimism. From the establishment of Telefís Éireann in 1962 various Irish-language organisations and politicians requested a separate television channel in Irish. In 1963 Conradh na Gaeilge passed a motion and sent a letter to Government requesting the establishment of a television channel in Irish on the edge of the Gaeltacht. Even during the demonstrations demanding a Gaeltacht radio channel, Coiste Práinne na Gaeilge, which was active during 1968–9, demanded a radio and television channel in Irish for the whole country.

During the 1960s the percentage of programmes in Irish on Telefís Éireann were so low that much of the focus of complaints was on that. Quite a few politicians and Irish-language organisations complained that 2% was too low. During the 1970s the disatisfaction with the quantity of programmes in Irish was tempered by the quality and the high ratings achieved by a number of programmes in Irish and bilingual programmes. *Féach* (current affairs) was achieving an audience of over 650,000 people, *Gairm* (studio interviews) an audience of 210,000, *Amuigh faoin Spéir* (nature) 780,000[63] and *Trom agus Eadrom* (chatshow – mostly in English) between 600,000 and 700,000.[64] It was in this context, as well as in the context of Irish speakers being considered a minority group with rights and with the success of RnaG, that demands began for a Gaeltacht television channel. In the Dáil the issue was raised on occasion. For example in the 'amendment debate' in 1975 Ciarán P. Murphy asked: 'Has any consideration been given to a possible television service for the Gaeltacht areas?'[65] Similarly, in 1979, Tom O'Donnell said:

> I am posing the question that perhaps now might be a good time to look at the possibility, which has been the dream of all involved in the language and the development of the Gaeltacht, of establishing a Gaeltacht television service.[66]

63 SD 79, 12 March 1975, col. 822.   **64** DD 294, 17 November, 1976, col. 121.   **65** DD 285, 28 October 1975, col. 480.   **66** DD 317, 4 December 1979, col. 663.

According to Hourigan, from the mid-1960s until the mid-1970s, Conradh na Gaeilge's main media campaign was to remonstrate with RTÉ for its lack of broadcasting in Irish.[67] After 1975, however, it also began to demand a separate television channel in Irish. It maintained both aspects – the demand for more programmes in Irish on RTÉ, in order to reach as many people as possible and keep the revival efforts alive, and the demand for a separate channel in Irish to serve the minority Irish-speaking population and help preserve the language where spoken.

At this stage much of the emphasis was on a separate television station for the Gaeltacht. Perhaps it is understandable, particularly after the commencement of RnaG, that the existing radio model could be imitated in television. Even at this stage, however, there was a tension emerging between what came to be known as the Teilifís na Gaeltachta and the Teilifís na Gaeilge models. The first was based on the RnaG model, with an emphasis on the Gaeltacht community. The second model presented the separate channel as a third national channel, which just happened to be in Irish.

In 1975 Conradh na Gaeilge organised a conference on Celtic minority-language broadcasting.[68] This conference, according to Hourigan, encouraged some young members of Conradh na Gaeilge to believe that a separate national Irish-language television channel was required and they engaged in radical tactics such as climbing RTÉ's broadcasting mast in December 1976, non-payment of television licence fees resulting in three people being imprisoned in 1977, and seven members of Conradh na Gaeilge chaining themselves to doors of the GPO (General Post Office) in March 1977. The model they advocated was the Teilifís na Gaeilge model. At Conradh na Gaeilge's national convention in the Connemara Gaeltacht in 1980 a motion was passed to campaign for a separate Irish-language television channel rather than for improvements in RTÉ's Irish-language broadcasting. Having this meeting in the Gaeltacht created a tentative link between the Teilifís na Gaeilge and Teilifís na Gaeltachta objectives. However, Conradh na Gaeilge did not focus solely on the television issue, they continued to lobby on a broader base, for example seeking a Bill of Rights for Irish speakers in 1985.

In the late 1970s a number of younger Irish-language activists began campaigning for a separate channel in Irish. The most radical demonstrations were organised by a group calling themselves 'Freagra' (Answer). As a wing of Conradh na Gaeilge, they also demanded increased broadcasting time in Irish on RTÉ. They wrote slogans on billboards across Dublin, organised sit-ins in RTÉ, intruded on an RTÉ news broadcast while chanting slogans; they also engaged in many other tactics and demonstrations.

---

67 N. Hourigan, op. cit., pp. 45–6.   68 N. Hourigan, 'Framing processes and the Celtic television campaigns', *Irish Journal of Sociology* 8 (1998), p. 58.

The demands for more programmes in Irish (whether on one of RTÉ's channels or on a separate station) were founded on the discourse of rights regarding Irish speakers, which developed throughout the 1970s and 1980s. This discourse, which had emerged from the tension between the two national identities, was used by Irish-language organisations to argue that Irish speakers have the right to be served in the language they have chosen to speak. Also, Irish has continued to be seen by the majority of Irish people as a central prop of national identity, as is evident from recent censuses and surveys.[69]

This discourse of minority rights and the tension between the old and the modern national identities were evident in two reports on Irish-language broadcasting written during this period. The first was that of the Advisory Committee on Irish Language Broadcasting appointed in March 1977 by RTÉ. This committee claimed that broadcasts in the Irish language were a personal right, that there was a large number of Irish speakers and that a large majority of the population agreed with the use of Irish on television and radio. These arguments could be termed minority-rights issues. One could argue that as it was RTÉ being addressed, the arguments were phrased in a language ideologically acceptable to it. Although RTÉ reflected a diversity of perspectives, many of the elements of the new national identity, such as an emphasis on market forces in audience figures, were evident. However, it also retained many elements of the traditional national identity. The arguments presented by this committee were not only phrased in the acceptable language of minority rights but were also strengthened by appealing to the 'popularity' of the language (i.e. popularity implies viewership). However, the recommendations of this committee were ignored by RTÉ and never published.[70]

Elements of the 'old' identity were evident in the arguments addressed to the Government by the Irishspeaking public through the second report, in 1987. The focus was more on arguments related to distinctiveness than on minority rights, e.g. 'that television impacts on the formation of attitudes and outlooks, and that we are at present being influenced greatly by programmes from abroad, and by the English language'.[71]

---

69 Cf. P. Ó Riagáin and M. Ó Gliasáin, op. cit.   **70** Cf. Working Group on Irish Language Television Broadcasting, *Report to the Ministers for the Gaeltacht and Communications* (Dublin: Government Stationery Office, 1987), p. 9.   **71** Ibid., p. 13.

Table 4.2: Schedule of programmes on RTÉ, 14–20 October 1985[72]

	RTÉ1		RTÉ2	
Monday	Dilín ó Deamhas		Nuacht	19.15–19.30
	[Children's Programme] 17.00–17.10			
	Iris '85 [Current Affairs]	21.30–22.00	Nuacht	19.15–19.30
Tuesday			Nuacht	19.15–19.30
Wednesday			Nuacht	19.15–19.30
Thursday			Nuacht	19.30–19.45
Friday			Nuacht	19.15–19.30
Saturday	Dilín ó Deamhas (repeat)		Nuacht	20.05–20.15
Sunday			Nuacht	20.00–20.10
		50 mins		95 mins
TOTAL				145 mins
Percentage of total broadcasting time				2.0

Both committees also made concrete recommendations to RTÉ. The Advisory Committee on the Irish Language's central proposition was that RTÉ should provide a full and varied range of programmes in Irish on RTÉ – its recommendations were not implemented by RTÉ. The Working Group on Irish Language Television Broadcasting made similar recommendations which were presented as a 'graduated approach towards improving Irish language programmes on television', accompanied by completion dates. A full range of Irish-language programmes, according to the Group, would comprise news and current affairs, magazine programmes, films and soundtracks in Irish, sport, bilingual programmes, educational programmes, learners 'programmes, features, drama, and religion.[73] Over the next few years (1987–91) there was little increase in the amount of time devoted to Irish-language broadcasting on RTÉ television.

Primarily, the options that were open to Irish-language television broadcasting were: first, that RTÉ assign a definite block of time on one channel for broadcasting through Irish; second, more Irish programmes could be assimilated into RTÉ's schedule and spread across both channels; the final option was to establish a separate Irish-language channel. The lower potential audience for programmes in Irish meant that RTÉ would not support any of these suggestions for fear of losing advertising revenue.[74] The Working

Group itself was also not in favour of a separate Irish-language channel for fear of ghettoising the language and felt it would be better to improve the state of Irish on RTÉ. Many others amongst the Irish-speaking community also expressed the concern that a separate Irish-language television channel would ghettoise the language. Some argued that the success of S4C in Wales and of Scottish Gaelic programmes were the result of being on bilingual stations.[75] However, it is clear that the recommendations of both committees were not implemented.

There was a lack of support for a separate channel in Irish; however, if RTÉ was unwilling to increase the amount of programmes in Irish on its channels, the only option appeared to be the establishment of a separate Irish-language television channel. Reg Hindley, in a rare moment, reflected the general mood amongst Irish speakers when he argued that 'an Irish-language television channel would in theory vastly assist the survival of the Gaeltacht by removing the major anglicizing influence on every child in every home'.[76] He went on to claim that an Irish-language television channel was 'unlikely to materialize'. Thus, Hindley argued that the 'best hope' was for improvements in Irish-language programming on RTÉ.

RTÉ had serious reservations about both the costs of producing more programmes in Irish and about the threat to its advertising revenue if programmes in Irish were broadcast and did not attract a large audience. Audience figures and advertising revenue are important for RTÉ. RTÉ has regarded Irish-language programmes as unpopular, claiming that

> While the Survey figures quoted in the Green Paper may indeed indicate a growth in favour of the language and, out of that, a perceived growth in the need for more and better programmes in Irish, the fact is that this does not translate into any growth in audiences for such programmes when they are transmitted.[77]

Some Irish speakers argued in response that RTÉ failed to tap fully the potential audience. They claimed that *Cúrsaí Ealaíne* (arts) outstripped its English language equivalent, *Black Box*, in the mid-1990s, and that Irish-language children's programmes such as *Dinín* and *Scéalaíocht Janosch* (Janosch's Storytelling), which were broadcast on *The Den* (children's afternoon schedule) achieved audiences of 250,000.[78] They also claimed that RTÉ had a limited vision of Irish speakers, visualising them stereotypically. RTÉ

---

75 Sianel Pedwar Cymru (S4C) is a Welsh-language station, but broadcasts a substantial proportion of English language programmes. Scottish-Gaelic programmes are broadcast on the two main English-language stations in Scotland. **76** R. Hindley, *The death of the Irish language* (London: Routledge 1990), p. 174. **77** RTÉ, *RTÉ Response to the Government's Green Paper on Broadcasting* (Dublin: RTÉ, 1995), p. 28. **78** J. Gogan, op. cit., p. 14.

visualised the audience as small and made no effort to attract a larger audience, thus creating a self-fulfilling prophecy – it broadcast cheap, special interest, talking-heads programmes on Network2, automatically ensuring a small audience and reinforcing audience perception of Irish-language programmes. RTÉ also visualised the audience for Irish-language programmes as a special interest group and therefore broadcast current affairs and arts programmes (and virtually no other type of programme) which dealt primarily with what RTÉ perceived to be 'Irish-language issues'. Kelly and Rolston argued that although Irish speakers are as diverse in their interests as non Irish speakers, they 'are seen as a group with special minority rights, and as constituting a specialist listenership group'.[79]

Regardless of the struggle to improve the situation on television, RnaG continued to be praised throughout the 1980s. During discussion of the Independent Local Broadcasting Authority Bill in 1983 a number of deputies argued in the Dáil that RTÉ would be badly affected by the emergence of local radio stations. A few argued that RnaG would be damaged by this competition. For example, Jim Mitchell stated that 'a further notable omission was any consideration of the effects of the Bill on the existing national broadcasting services provided by RTÉ, including Radio na Gaeltachta'[80] and John Donnellan argued that

> RTÉ at present provide three national radio channels, including Radio na Gaeltachta. New independent services must clearly have some effect on the existing networks. It would have been reasonable to expect the promoters of this Bill to offer some comment on that aspect, but they have not done so.[81]

The following year (on 4 April 1984) RTÉ applied for permission to extend its radio broadcasting hours, including RnaG. It wanted an extra few hours on RnaG in the morning Monday–Friday. The following year the Minister for Communications, Jim Mitchell,[82] gave RTÉ permission to extend RnaG's broadcasting hours. The longer broadcasting hours started on Easter Monday 1986.

Further increases in the number of hours of broadcasting on RnaG came during the debate on the Sound Broadcasting Bill in 1987–8. Ray Burke[83] announced that he had given permission for

79 M. Kelly and B. Rolston, 'Broadcasting in Ireland: issues of national identity and censorship', in P. Clancy et al. (eds), *Irish society: sociological perspectives* (Dublin: Institute of Public Administration, 1995), p. 575.   **80** DD 343, 14 June 1983, col. 1432.   **81** Ibid., 15 June 1983, col. 1736.   **82** Jim Mitchell was Minister for Communications, 1984–7.   **83** Ray Burke was Minister for Communications, 1987–91.

an extra 1,092 hours per annum to enable the Radio na Gaeltachta service to broadcast continuously throughout the day ... The effect of that will be that Radio na Gaeltachta, on Mondays to Fridays – instead of their present practice of broadcasting from 8 a.m. to 1.30 p.m. and from 5 p.m. to 8 p.m. – will be able to broadcast from 8 a.m. to 8 p.m. On Saturdays they broadcast at present from 11 a.m. to 1.30 p.m. and from 5 p.m. to 8 p.m. but in future they will be able to broadcast on Saturdays from 11 a.m. right through to 8 p.m. At present they broadcast on Sundays from 11 a.m. to 1 p.m. and from 5 p.m. to 8 p.m.[84]

He went on to praise RnaG:

> This service has carved out a very important niche in the cultural life of the country. I know that the improved service which the station will be able to offer will be greatly welcomed not just by the people of the Gaeltachtaí but also by the strong and loyal listeners to that service throughout the country to whom the Irish language is of great importance.[85]

A few months earlier, debating this Bill, the Minister had argued that applicants for a local community radio licence covering any Gaeltacht area would be expected to demonstrate a contribution to preserving Irish as a spoken language.[86] As the debate continued quite a few other speakers echoed the opinion that local community radio stations should represent Irish identity and should broadcast programmes in Irish.

Similar arguments were made during the debate of the Broadcasting Bill in 1990. For example, Joe Costello claimed that

> The proliferation of independent stations around Gaeltacht areas will encroach on Raidió na Gaeltachta. That will be a further threat to the language. I would like to hear the Minister's comments on that and whether licences will be given to stations in areas bordering the Gaeltachtaí without the constraints of promoting the Irish language.[87]

In June 1988, there was a criticism which echoed criticisms of Cruise O'Brien's amendment, more than a decade earlier, of the RTÉ Authority's statutory responsibility to implement the State's language policy. This criticism from Proinsías de Rossa was contained in a proposed replacement, in the Bill, of the statement 'the extent to which programmes in the Irish language or programmes relating to Irish culture are to be provided', with the more explicit statement 'the quantity, quality, range and type of programmes in the

84 DD 381, 1 June 1988, cols 888–9.   **85** Ibid.   **86** DD 376, 8 December 1987, cols 1193–1202.
87 SD 126, 18 July 1990, col. 720.

Irish language and the extent of programmes relating to Irish culture proposed to be provided'. The Minister's response began, in a vein that perfectly
mimicked Cruise O'Brien's in the mid-1970s – 'this is unnecessary because the
element which the amendment introduces relating to the quality, range and
type of such programmes is embraced by the preceding criteria'. He continued, however, in a manner that represented the continuing vigour of the
earlier ideology – 'Nonetheless, in view of the commitment of all sides of the
House to the encouragement of the language and culture, I am prepared to
accept the amendment as put forward by Deputy de Rossa.'[88]

A few years later an Irish-language local community radio station was
established in Dublin. Raidió na Life began broadcasting in 1993 and claims
a listenership of 13,000. Raidió na Life was founded by Comharchumann
Raidió Átha Cliath Teoranta and is staffed by volunteers. In its application
to the IRTC (the Independent Radio and Television Commission) it claimed
that its audience was 'Irish speakers of all ages, people interested in alternative music. Core audience of 14,000 in Dublin' and that its programme
policy was 'to reflect the broad range of interest of an urban population: –
music alternative, Irish & European rock, traditional, jazz, classical and
world: Talk: business, current affairs, environmental, local, international
events, sports, arts etc. all through Irish' (www.irtc.ie). Its broadcasting
hours are 4.30 p.m. to midnight on Monday-Friday and noon to midnight
at the weekend. In 1999 Raidió na Life was awarded a contract renewal for
a further five years.

A Gaeltacht television station?
The strength of the demands for a separate Irish-language channel continued
to increase throughout the 1980s and, according to Ó Feinneadha, these
demands were a continuation of demands for more programmes in the Irish
language on RTÉ.[89] In 1980, at the same time as Conradh na Gaeilge had
decided to demand a separate Irish-language television channel (the Teilifís
na Gaeilge model) rather than more Irish-language programmes on RTÉ,
'Coiste ar son Teilifís Gaeltachta' (Committee for Gaeltacht television – the
Teilifís na Gaeltachta model) was instituted by Irish-language activists resident in the Gaeltacht, such as Ciarán Ó Feinneadha, Seosamh Ó Cuaig, Seán
Ó Drisceoil and Donncha Ó hÉalaithe. They tried to replicate the RnaG
campaign by setting up a pirate station, but unfortunately a technician died
suddenly and the project ended. Ó hÉalaithe and others who had been
involved in the Gaeltacht civil rights movement felt that there were not
enough programmes in Irish on RTÉ and

---

88 DD 381, 1 June 1988, cols 1104–8.   **89** C. Ó Feinneadha, 'TnaG – an ród a bhí romhainn',
Comhar 54:5 (1995), p. 10.

chonaic muid an dream a bhí faoi mhíbhuntáiste ná seo iad pobal na Gaeltachta a raibh an cultúr áitiúil cineál préambaithe go huile agus go hiomlán i nGaeilge go leanúnach leis na céadta bliain agus go raibh sé ag teacht chuig an bpointe nach raibh ag éirí leis an bpobal sin an teanga a chur go dti an chéad glún eile mar *just* bhí paistí ag diúltú. Bhí *reaction* uafásach ó pháistí sna hochtóidí in aghaidh na Gaeilge, *just* bhíodar ag diúltú – chomh luath agus a d'fhoghlaimidís Béarla dhiúltóidís Gaeilge a labhairt.[90]

(we saw that the group which was disadvantaged was the Gaeltacht public whose culture was kind of totally and completely rooted in the Irish language continuously for hundreds of years and that it was reaching a point when that community was unable to pass the language on because children just were refusing. There was a terrible reaction from children in the eighties against the Irish language, they were just refusing – as soon as they would learn English they'd refuse to speak Irish).

They felt that campaigning for an increase in Irish-language programmes on RTÉ would be fruitless, because, as Ó hÉalaithe said, 'Níl ansin ach seafóid … ní bhfaigh idh mnid sin go deo, tá sé trialta sách minic'[91] ('That's just rubbish … we'd never get that, it's been tried often enough'). They decided, under the new name 'Meitheal Oibre Theilifís na Gaeltachta' (Teilifís na Gaeltachta cooperaive), to attempt a trial broadcast as a Gaeltacht channel. Donncha Ó hÉalaithe, Ruairi Ó Tuairisc and Pádraig de Bhaldraithe went to visit a station in the Faroe Islands which broadcast at low cost and, from what they learned, they were able to broadcast eighteen hours of pre-recorded and live material illegally from Ros Muc, Co. Galway on 2–5 November 1987. Ó hÉalaithe tells the story:

> Ar an mbealach ar ais dhúinn chas an triúir againn le Bob Quinn ar an traein anuas ó Bhleá Cliath agus chuir sé ceist simplí orm – 'An gceapann sibh gur féidir é a dhéanamh i gConamara? 'agus dúirt mise 'Is cinnte gur féidir.' '*OK*,' dúirt sé, 'déanfaidh muid é.' *So* chuaigh mé ar ais abhaile agus rinne mé dearmad air agus 'chéad rud eile fuair mé glao gutháin thart ar mí Lúnasa ó Bob Quinn ag rá go raibh duine aimsithe aige a bhí sásta *transmitters* a thógáil agus go gcosnódh sé ceithre mhíle punt agus dúirt sé', 'An féidir leat ceithre mhíle punt a bhailiú taobh istigh de coicís?' *What do you do with a challenge like that? You can't say, 'I can't collect the money.'* *So* bhailíomar cúig mhíle, 's tógadh na

90 D. Ó hÉalaithe, in a personal interview with the author on 11 April 1997.   **91** Ibid.

transmitters, agus Mí Dheireadh Fómhair ansin cuireamar an stáisiún brabach seo ar an aer thar deireadh seachtaine i Ros Muc le linn Oireachtas na nGael[92] agus i ndáiríre is craoladh beo den chuid is mó a bhí ann *just* mar gheall ar bhí imeachtaí ar siúl agus bhí dhá *cameras* againn agus bhíomar ag craoladh beo – ag *switch* áil ó *camera* amháin go dtí *camera* eile agus bhí sé sin ag dul amach ar *radius* thart ar cúig mhíle dhéag amach ó Ros Muc agus bhí *signal* iontach le fáil ag daoine comh maith le RTÉ haon nó dó. *So*, ar ndóigh, thug sé sin an-dóchas ar fad dúinn, mar roimhe sin bhí daoine ag rá, *Look*, 'Tá sé róchostasach, ní féidir é a dhéanamh' agus mar sin de. D'athraigh an deireadh seachtaine sin an bonn argóna.[93]

(On our way back the three of us met Bob Quinn on the train from Dublin and he asked me a simple question, 'Do you think it's possible to do it in Conamara?' and I said, 'It's certainly possible.' he said, 'we'll do it.' So I went back home and I forgot it and the next thing, around August, I got a phone call from Bob Quinn saying that he'd located a person who was happy to build the transmitters and that it'd cost four thousand pounds and he said, 'Can you collect four thousand pounds within a fortnight?' What do you do with a challenge like that? You can't just say, 'I can't collect the money.' So we collected five thousand, and the transmitters were built, and November then we put this pirate station on the air over a weekend in Ros Muc during Oireachtas na nGael[94] and really it was live broadcasting for the most part because events were happening and we had two cameras and we were broadcasting live – switching from one camera to another camera – and that was going out for a radius of about fifteen miles out from Ros Muc and people were getting a wonderful signal as well as RTÉ 1 or 2. So, of course, that gave us all confidence, because before this people were saying, 'Look, it's too expensive, it can't be done,' and so forth. That weekend changed the debate.)

They broadcast more programmes in December 1988, when there was a pirate broadcasting amnesty.

The following year Meitheal Oibre Theilifís na Gaeltachta got together with Dublin-based activists to form a national coalition of groups and individuals, which they called FNT (Feachtas Náisinnta Teilifíse – National Television Campaign). Ó Feinneadha, who was part of FNT and had been

---

92 Saor Raidió Chonamara had also broadcast illegally during Oireachtas na nGael almost two decades before as part of the campaign for RnaG.   93 Ibid.   94 Saor Raidió Chonamara had also broadcast illegally during Oireachtas na nGael almost two decades before as part of the campaign for RnaG.

involved in the first efforts to broadcast illegally in 1980, said that he did not agree with the division between the campaigns for Teilifís na Gaeltachta and for Teilifís na Gaeilge, he said, 'Sé sin le rá nár aontaíos leis an meon gur chóir Bealach Áitiúil Gaeltachta a chur ar bun, go díreach mar nár aontaigh mé leis na daoine i mBaile Átha Cliath a bhí ag iarraidh Teilifís na Gaeilge a bhunú agus gan aird na aitheantas ceart a thabhairt do na pobail Gaeltachta'[95] ('That is to say, I did not agree with the notion that there should be a local Gaeltacht channel, just as I did not agree with the people in Dublin who wanted to establish Teilifís na Gaeilge and give no proper recognition to the Gaeltacht communities'). It was under FNT that the Dublin-based Teilifís na Gaeilge movement merged with the Connemara-based Teilifís na Gaeltachta movement.

---

95 C. Ó Feirmeadha, op. cit., p. 13.

CHAPTER 5

The foundation of Teilifís na Gaeilge

The main thrust of the campaign that led to TnaG occurred in the early 1990s. By that time the modern ideology had shifted, because of failure to achieve a number of national objectives such as restoring the Irish language, uniting the island and creating sufficient employment to stem the tide of emigration. The emergence of the modern ideology had been based on its critique of the failure of the earlier ideology to achieve its national objectives. Although, economically, Ireland went through a modernisation phase from the 1960s onward, it was clear by the early 1980s that there were serious economic problems and the violence in the North continued unabated. By this stage a new ideology had emerged on the international stage. The world had seen the advent of neoliberalism in Thatcherism, Reaganomics and the various structural adjustment programmes imposed on indebted nations. The global economy had become neoliberal and Ireland sought a niche in this economy, which it found, at least temporarily, in the 1990s, and was dubbed 'the Celtic Tiger'. The modern ideology, which had been quite liberal, was overtaken by a neoliberal and, to a certain extent, postmodern ideology.

The role of the State diminished with the shift from one ideology to the next. During the traditional nation-building ideology in the early years, the State took it upon itself to construct, promote and preserve a particular version of Irish national identity. Especially from the 1930s, the State also played an interventionist, protectionist role in the economy. During the period of the modern ideology, its promoters argued that the State should not intervene in matters of personal choice, such as issues of identity, except to ensure equality and freedom of choice. Identity was regarded a personal matter. One could argue that this was the individualisation of identity. The economic version of this ideology was Keynesian and involved the construction of the welfare state. To a certain extent it was about the State intervening to ensure more equality. During this period the State began to look toward Europe; this was the case particularly after joining the European Economic Community on 1 January 1973.

In more recent years the Irish State has sought a niche in the global economy and has had to adapt to its conditions. Within this ideology the State is expected to be even more *laisser faire* than before and not only is there a continuation of the individualisation of identity, there is also an individualisation of the economy. Mary Kelly maintained of the late 1980s and early 1990s that

> The focus on the nation state and the privileged position of national public service broadcasting have been undermined by privatization, commercialization and internationalization. Underlying this is an ideology of competitive individualism and letting market forces reign supreme.[1]

Supporters of the modern and more recent ideology often emphasised democratic principles such as equality and choice (see discussions, above, of Fitzgerald and the '*Late Late Show* debate' and also Cruise O'Brien and the 'amendment debate').

These democratic principles are embodied in citizenship. T.H. Marshall argued that citizenship was primarily about rights – civil, political and social rights – such as freedom of speech, of faith, to own property, to engage in contracts, and to justice; the right to participate in politics as elected or voter; and economic welfare and security rights, as well as participation in the 'social heritage'.[2] B.S. Turner also added cultural citizenship.[3] To a large extent citizenship is a different method of including individuals in society based on achieving the criteria of the status of citizenship rather than on possessing certain characteristics. David Held argued that

> If citizenship entails membership in the community and membership in the community implies forms of social participation, then citizenship is above all about the involvement of people in the community in which they live.[4]

The increasing emphasis on citizenship since the 1960s has been an alternative to the solidarity of national identity. Participation by citizens occurs in the public sphere, and the mass media have come to be the prominent institution of the public sphere.[5] Thus, for many proponents of the modern and

1 M. Kelly, op. cit, p. 83.   2 T.H. Marshall, 'Citizenship and social class' in T.H. Marshall and Tom Bottomore, *Citizenship and social class* (London: Pluto Press, 1992).   3 B.S. Turner, 'Outline of a theory of citizenship', *Sociology* 24:2 (1990).   4 D. Held, 'Between State and civil society: citizenship' in G. Andrews (ed.), *Citizenship* (London: Lawrence and Wishart, 1991), p. 20.   5 Cf. J. Habermas, 1989, op. cit., for a detailed discussion of the concept of the public sphere.

recent ideology, the availability of choice of television channels etc. is a principle of citizenship.

Discussing the concept of the public sphere, the author of the Green Paper on Broadcasting asked:

> Should there be a single, generalised public sphere in any state or is it more useful, in countries incorporating ethnic and/or linguistic communities, rather than the single language nation state, to think of a minority public sphere existing inside or alongside the dominant one?[6]

From this there is a suggestion that TnaG would be another choice for citizens. In its unpublished response to the Green Paper[7] TnaG argued that one of the main points on which its philosophy is based is 'tuiscint nua ar fhéiniúlacht tré ghuth a thabhairt don phobal' ('a new understanding of identity by giving a voice to the public') and 'is cuid dhílis de bhunfhealsúnacht an Pháipéir Ghlais gurb é an saoránach féin, an ghnáth-thomhaltóir craolacháin an té is mó a bhfuil gá lena chearta a chosaint go láidir más fúinn ról gníomhach a thabhairt dó sa todhchaí chraolacháin' ('it is a basic part of the Green Paper's philosophy that it is the citizen's, the ordinary viewer's, rights which must be protected if we are to provide him/her with an active role in the future of broadcasting').

Before TnaG began broadcasting it organised a series of meetings throughout the country. These meetings were open to the public to discuss any issues relevant to TnaG and represented an interesting development in Ireland, relating to public access to public broadcasting. Moreover, the structure of TnaG, as a commissioning body, was expected to provide the public with programmes produced by a variety of independent producers with different perspectives. Although this does not constitute public access, the philosophy behind it is that by offering access to broadcasting to a range of different producers the public is presented with a variety of viewpoints, thus taking a step in the direction of averting consensus management.

As well as being coupled to citizenship and democracy, the media continued to be of relevance to identity. The fledgling Irish State had employed radio to promote Irish national identity, but more recently Heller et al. argued that

> identities are not supplied by immediate experience or feelings, and
> the themes are not present in the experience and memories of the

6 Department of Arts, Culture and the Gaeltacht, *Active or passive? Broadcasting in the future tense: Green Paper on Broadcasting* (Dublin: Government Stationery Office, 1995), p. 203. 7 TnaG, *Páipéar Glas an Rialtais ar Chraolachán: Freagra Theilifís na Gaeilge* (Dublin: TnaG, 1995) (The Government's Green Paper on Broadcasting: Teilifís na Gaeilge's Response).

participants as an immediate reflection of events and encounters. They need to be elaborated, transformed, and legitimated through public communication, taking into account existing themes and identities and working upon them with resources available to the participants. More importantly, all this must happen publicly, the 'grammar' of public communication having characteristics significantly different from those of private communication.[8]

Campaigners for a separate television channel in Irish were able to continue to argue that Irish speakers are a minority of national importance, insofar as they preserve Irish, and Irish has continued to be believed, by the majority of the population, to be a significant symbol of national identity. These campaigners were also able to draw on the more recent ideologies to argue that Irish speakers as Irish citizens had the right to choose to be informed and entertained in Irish and that it was also their democratic right to have access to an Irish-language public sphere in the form of a separate television channel in Irish.

A major flaw in this 'postmodern' ideology is that it has a very passive notion of citizenship, which almost equates the citizen with the consumer. The thesis that citizens have a right to freedom of choice is based on the notion of an election in which voters have a choice of candidates – just as citizens get to vote for the candidate of their choice, they also get to watch the programmes of their choice, speak the language of their choice, to choose their own identity and to choose from a range of products in shops. Within this ideology the market begins to look like an election, but in an election a candidate who fails to achieve the quota is unelected, just as a company which fails to sell its product goes out of business. Minorities have rights, but only if they are large minorities. Although Irish speakers form a large minority, Ireland is too small a market to support four television channels on advertising revenue alone. Fortunately for the campaigners for a separate Irish-language television channel, they had another ideology on which to draw and they had supporters in positions of power.

Getting on the agenda
The television channel, TnaG, which emerged, was not pre-existent waiting for the right moment to come into being. It resulted from the actions (and the interaction) of individuals within institutions such as government, the civil service, RTÉ and Feachtas Náisiúnta Teilifíse. The form the channel took was also influenced by the nexus from which it emerged.

8 M. Heller, D. Nemedi and R. Rényi, 'Structural changes in the Hungarian public sphere under State socialism', *Comparative Social Research* 4 (1994), pp. 69–70.

The decision to establish a separate Irish-language television channel seemed to enter the agenda through a series of stages. Four ministers were involved in the lead up to TnaG. They were Charles Haughey, Minister for the Gaeltacht (and Taoiseach – the Minister for Communications at the time was Ray Burke); Séamus Brennan, Minister for Communications;[9] Máire Geoghegan-Quinn, Minister for Communications;[10] and Michael D. Higgins, Minister for Arts, Culture and the Gaeltacht. The first two were incidental, while the latter two were central, to the establishment of TnaG.

It was during the late 1980s that Haughey expressed an interest in Irish-language broadcasting. The origin of TnaG can be traced to this period. Haughey commissioned a number of reports. However, this appeared to be a delaying or avoidance tactic. The first was the Working Group on Irish Language Broadcasting (1987) and the second was a report by Údarás na Gaeltachta (the Gaeltacht Authority), which is still unpublished. Ciarán Ó Feinneadha (a member of FNT) claimed that

> ní dearna Haughey faic, ach, ag an am céanna, i mo chroí istigh tá mé ag tabhairt an *benefit of the doubt* dó. B'eisean Taoiseach na tíre agus bhí sé sásta a rá '*Well*, tá mise ar a shon'. *Now*, dháiríre, ó thaobh misnigh de ba rud tábhachtach é sin, *now*, ó thaobh briseadh mhisnigh de ba rud uafásach é nach ndearna sé aon dul chun cinn.[11]

> (Haughey did nothing, yet, at the same time, in my heart I give him the benefit of the doubt. He was the Taoiseach of the country and he was willing to say, 'well, I'm in favour of it'. Now, really, in terms of courage it was an important thing, now, in terms of discouragement it was a terrible thing that he made no headway).

Under Charles Haughey, as Minister for the Gaeltacht and Taoiseach, the idea of a separate channel gained acceptance. In late 1987 he promised IR£500,000 (€635,000) from the National Lottery to go towards a separate Irish-language channel. This was against the advice he received from the report he had commissioned,[12] which concluded that the establishment of a separate channel in Irish was inadvisable at that time. Although the arguments for a separate channel received support from Haughey, no concrete steps were taken – the money he promised was not assigned to this project and four years later the Minister for Finance, Albert Reynolds (later Taoiseach), claimed that

9 Seamus Brennan was Minister for Tourism, Transport and Communications, 1991–2. **10** Máire Geoghegan-Quinn was Minister for Tourism, Transport and Communications, February–November 1992. **11** C. Ó Feinneadha, in a personal interview with the author on 25 August 1998. **12** The author of this report was the 'Working Group on Irish Language Television Broadcasting', see p. 79, note 70, above.

due to cut-backs this money still could not be assigned (even though it was to come from the National Lottery and not from Government funds).

Late in 1988 Haughey commissioned Údarás na Gaeltachta to undertake a feasibility study. In July 1989 he said that the establishment of an Irish-language service was one of the top priorities of the new Government.[13] During the following few years Haughey and the Minister of State in the Department of the Gaeltacht (Pat 'the Cope' Gallagher) claimed that this report as well as recommendations from various organisations were being examined. At the Fianna Fáil Party Árd Fheis, on 9 March 1991 Haughey said in his Presidential Address that the television service would be established the following year, and Gallagher reiterated this in the Dáil two days later.

During his period in office Haughey made promises and established committees. Although these are stereotypical political delaying tactics, they set the agenda for the future – that increases in television programmes in Irish would happen as a result of establishing a separate channel in Irish and not through the existing two RTÉ television channels. There was also an indication that the separate channel would follow the Teilifís na Gaeilge and not the Teilifís na Gaeltachta model. An advisory committee, set up by Haughey, under the chairmanship of Proinsías Mac Aonghusa (former President of Conradh na Gaeilge) recommended that a separate channel be based in the Rath Cairn Gaeltacht near Dublin.[14] This suggested that although it would have a Gaeltacht element, its proximity to Dublin implied a model that differed from the RnaG model.

In 1990 the Minister for Communications (Ray Burke) brought the Broadcasting Bill before the Oireachtas. It was clear that many advocates of a separate Irish-language television channel presumed that it would be based on the RnaG model. During the debate Ted Nealon argued that the Bill would place two major obstacles in the way of the establishment of a Gaeltacht television channel. He claimed that it would be impossible to have a Gaeltacht television channel if the third domestic television band was allocated to a commercial station (TV3) and that RTÉ's financial capacity to fund a separate Gaeltacht television channel would be seriously undermined if its advertising revenue was 'capped' (i.e. a limit placed on the amount of advertising revenue RTÉ would be allowed to earn).[15] Michael D. Higgins then stated that

> What we are now witnessing is a total abandonment of the right of the
> people of the Gaeltachts to have a television station located in the

---

13 Haughey made this statement before he had even received the report from Údarás na Gaeltachta, which arrived a few months later in September 1989. 14 This information comes from N. Ó Gadhra, in a personal interview with the author on 11 April 1997. 15 DD 401, 11 July 1990, cols 1219–50.

Gaeltacht which meet their own needs and provides a national service for anyone interested in the language. There is no point in imagining that this is not the position.[16]

The following day in the Seanad the Minister stated that he had retained enough UHF frequencies to have both TV3 and TnaG. In that statement the Minister said that

> There have been some uninformed suggestions that the proposal to allow the third television channel to establish its own UHF transmission system rules out the possibility of establishing a Teilifís na Gaeltachta, should a decision to that effect be taken.[17]

Pól Ó Foighil seized on this statement to point out an inconsistency between the Minister's statement and the Taoiseach's promise of a Gaeltacht channel:

> Is é an clásal deiridh – 'should a decision to that effect be taken' – a chuireann imní ormsa. Sin iad focail an Aire féin ach ba é an Taoiseach a dúirt go mbeadh seirthís teilifíse Gaeltachta ann, agus dhearbhaigh sé faoi dhó é, go poiblí, ar Raidió Éireann. Má dhúirt, cén fáth a bhfuil an ráiteas sin i gcáipéis an Aire atá os ar gcomhair inniu? An amhlaidh go raibh an Taoiseach ag caint as bealach?[18]

> (It is the last clause – 'should a decision to that effect be taken' – that worries me. They are the Minister's own words but it was the Taoiseach who said that there would be a Gaeltacht television service, and he confirmed it twice, publicly, on Radio Éireann. Why is that statement in the Minister's document before us today? Was the Taoiseach in fact talking out of turn?)

After all the promises and advisory bodies, the National Lottery funds which Haughey had vaguely 'earmarked' for the Irish-language television service were directed to the state coffers and later that year (1991) Haughey said on Raidió na Gaeltachta that due to financial constraints he was uncertain as to whether or not the television channel would be established. Soon afterwards Haughey lost the leadership of Fianna Fáil and left the political scene.

It was during this period that the Gaeltacht campaign joined forces with campaigners outside the Gaeltacht and thus began Feachtas Náisiúnta Teilifíse (FNT) as a national campaign. Donncha Ó hÉalaithe explained:

---

16 Ibid. Interestingly, Higgins went on to establish TnaG and revoke the 'cap'. **17** SD 126, 12 July 1990, col. 290. **18** Ibid., col. 414.

Lean muid ag caint le Bob Collins.[19] Seo, is dóiche, an tarna duine ba thábhachtaí in RTÉ, murab é an duine ba thábhachtaí agus choinnigh sé ar an eolas muid agus choinnigh mnide eisean ar an eolas agus ag pointe amháin dúirt sé liomsa '*Well look now*, sé an rud is tábhachtaí i ndáiríre ná go ndéanfaí an feachtas a leathnú amach go náisiúnta.' Chas mé le Ciarán Ó Feínneadha thíos in Inis agus shocraíomar gur mba chóir iarracht a dhéanamh an feachtas a leathnú taoth amuigh de Chonamara. *So* bhí cruinniú agam i mBleá Cliath agus is cuimhneach liom Pádraig Ó Snodaigh a bheith ann, Tomás Mac Síomóin, Ciarán Ó Feinneadha, táim ag ceapadh Liam Ó Cuinneagáin. *So* shocraíomar go ndéanfadh muid Feachtas Náisiúnta Teilifíse a bhunú.[20]

(We continued talking to Bob Collins.[21] Here's, I suppose, the second most important person in RTÉ, if not the most important and he kept us informed and we kept him informed and at one point he said to me 'Well look now, the most important thing really to do is to broaden the campaign nationally.' I met Ciarán Ó Feinneadha down in Ennis and we decided that we should attempt to broaden the campaign outside Connemara. So I had a meeting in Dublin and I remember Pádraig Ó Snodaigh was there, Tomás Mac Síomóin, Ciarán Ó Feinneadha, I think Liam Ó Cuinneagáin. So we decided we'd set up Feachtas Náisiúnta Teilifíse.)

Donncha Ó hÉalaithe, who lives in the Gaeltacht, and Ciarán Ó Feinneadha, who lives in Dublin, were founding members of FNT, both had been Irish-language activists since the 1970s and have been quite radical at times as is clear from statements such as:

ach ansin naoi déag ochtó sé, ní raith mórán cláracha Gaeilge ar RTÉ agus bhí roinnt daoine ag dul i bpriosún an uair sin mar gheall ar nach raibh siad ag íoc ceadúnas. Níor íoc mise aon cheadúnas ach faraor! níor tógadh mé ach oiread.[22]

(but then nineteen eighty-six, there weren't many Irish-language programmes on RTÉ and some people were going to prison that time because they weren't paying the licence. I didn't pay any licence but alas! I wasn't taken either).

19 Bob Collins, who is currently the Director-General of RTÉ, was Director of Television Programmes at the time.   **20** D. Ó hÉallaithe, op. cit.   **21** Bob Collins was Director of Television Programmes at the time.   **22** Ibid.

Hourigan points out that 'the state altered the broadcasting legislation in 1987. Henceforth, TV owners would have to pay a licence fee regardless of the specific station or the type of service they received'. She went on to claim that 'this effectively undermined any legal basis to the Irish language movement's case against RTÉ'.[23] However, Ó Feinneadha was arrested and imprisoned in 1992 for refusing to pay the television licence fee, in protest at the neglect of the Irish language by RTÉ.

Although other Irish-language groups such as Gael-Linn and Conradh na Gaeilge had included improvements in Irish-language broadcasting as part of their wider demands, and they became members of the FNT umbrella group. FNT also produced a list of supporters which included a few bishops, Mary Robinson (later to become President of Ireland), and Kader Asmal (a minister in the South African government, former law lecturer in Trinity College Dublin and founder of the Irish Anti-Apartheid movement in the 1960s). This gave FNT certain credibility. Had the various groups been actively involved in campaigning, FNT might have had to negotiate with them. However, the other Irish-language organisations supported FNT as an umbrella pressure group and allowed it to operate *solas*.

After Haughey, came Seamus Brennan as Minister for Communication in 1991–2. Brennan was uninterested in Irish-language broadcasting. Ciaran Ó Feinneadha claimed that Brennan would not meet FNT and that he quoted discouragingly large figures for the cost of building and running a separate Irish-language television channel.[24] Moreover, Ó Ciardha (who was appointed by Geoghegan-Quinn and later Higgins to advise on broadcasting in Irish) said that he was 'aire nach raibh an cháil air a raith an oiread sin [i] luí aige leis an nGaeilge'[25] ('a minister who did not have a reputation for having much of an inclination toward the Irish language').

During Haughey's and Brennan's eras FNT sent letters to all the TDs,[26] explaining their position; Ó hÉalaithe assisted Michael D. Higgins (in opposition) with speeches and questions for Question Time in the Dáil; FNT also held public meetings, in a hotel near the Dáil, and invited all the TDs; they also made contacts with the media and wrote letters to newspapers. Ó Feinneadha summarised their activities:

> rinneamar taighde, rinneamar a lán PR, rinneamar a lán stocaireacht, choinníomar i dteangmháil leanúnach le polaiteoirí sna páirtithe ar fad agus rinneamar forbairt ar an rud ó thaobh na heacnamaíochta de chomh maith.[27]

23 N. Hourigan, 2001, op. cit., pp. 53–4.   24 C. Ó Feinneadha, 1998, op. cit.   25 P. Ó Ciardha, in a personal interview with the author on 11 June 1998.   26 TD, or Teachta Dála, is a member of the Dáil.   27 C. Ó Feinneadha, 1998, op. cit.

Table 5.1: Schedule of programmes on RTÉ, 9–15 October 1995[28]

	RTÉ1		Network2	
Monday	Cinnlínte Nuacht [*News Headlines*]	13.20–13.22	Dinín [Children's Programme]	15.30–15.45
			Nuacht	20.30–20.38
Tuesday	Cinnlínte Nuacht	13.20–13.22	Tír na hÓige [*Land of Youth*]	15.20–15.40
			Cúrsaí Reatha [*Current Affairs*]	20.03–20.30
			Nuacht	20.03–20.30
Wednesday	Cinnlínte Nuacht	13.20–13.22	Cinnlínte Nuacht	18.55–19.00
	Teach i Iarusaileim [*A Hoase in Jeruasalem*]			
Thursday	Cinnlínte Nuacht	13.20–13.22	Scéalaíocht Janosch [*Janosch's Storytelling*]	15.20–15.40
			Tinteán [*Fireside*]	20.03–20.30
			Nuacht	20.30–20.38
Friday	Cinnlínte Nuacht	13.20–13.22	Mire Mara	15.25–15.50
			Nuacht	20.30–20.38
			Now You're Talkin	20.38–21.00
Saturday	Cinnlínte Nuacht	13.20–13.22	Nuacht	18.55–19.00
	Cúrsaí Ealaíne [*Art Affairs*]	23.10–23.40		
Sunday	Eureka (teenage magazine programme)	17.30–18.00	Nuacht	18.55–19.00
		80 mins		183 mins
	TOTAL			263 mins
	Percentage of total broadcasting time:			2.0

(we conducted research, we did a lot of PR, we did a lot of campaigning, we stayed in continual contact with politicians in all the parties and
we developed the thing from the economic side of it as well).

28 This table is based on research, by the author, of television schedules for October 1995.

Ó Feinneadha went on to emphasise their role in public relations. FNT also monitored newspapers. Ó Feinneadha provided examples of articles, which they perceived to be 'negative', in a number of newspapers such as the *Sunday Business Post*, the *Sunday Tribune*, the *Irish Independent*, and the *Irish Times*, to which FNT demanded a right of reply. Ó Feinneadha claimed that through their efforts they had brought the *Sunday Business Post*, the *Irish Times* and the *Evening Herald* around to their side and countered articles which he termed 'hatchet-jobs' or 'contemptible'. Most of this work appears to have been carried out independently by individual members of FNT's executive committee, especially Ó Feinneadha and Ó hÉalaithe, without the need for regular meetings.

They lobbied all the major political parties, with the result that in the following elections in the early 1990s all the major parties expressed support, in their election manifestos, for a separate Irish-language television channel. They established a relationship with civil servants in the Department of Communications. The civil servants were a source of information for FNT and Ó Feinneadha gathered as much information as possible from them. One example of the type of information Ó Feinneadha gained was a breakdown of the costs of providing a separate Irish-language channel. This breakdown clarified that the figure quoted by the Minister (Seamus Brennan) was large because it included the cost of purchasing land on top of mountains for aerials and purchasing land on the side of mountains for access to such aerials.[29] Ó Feinneadha said that a civil servant told him that this cost was not necessary because RTÉ's aerials could be used. He stated that

> is cuimhin liom timpeall 1991, don chéad uair, bhíomar ag plé le fadhbanna maidir le figiúirí agus bhí duine ag rá 'Cá bhfaigheann tú an t-eolas seo?' agus bhí muid ag rá', 'Is dóigh go bhfuil sé sa Roinn ach ní thabharfaidh siad dúinn é', agus caithfidh mé a rá, phioc mé suas an fón agus ghlaoigh mé ar an Roinn Cumarsáide, agus an bhean seo (ní chuimhin liom a sloinne) chaith sí timpeall uair an chloig ag míniú an rud dom, gach rud, ach bhí an bhean iontach ar fad.[30]

> (I remember around 1991, for the first time, we were dealing with problems with regard to figures and somebody just was saying, 'Where do you get this information?' and we were saying, 'I suppose it is in the Department, but they won't give it to us,' and I must say, I picked up the phone and I called the Department of Communications, and this woman (I don't remember her surname) spent about an hour

29 Ibid.   30 Ibid.

explaining the thing to me, everything, but the woman was absolutely wonderful.)

Thereafter they sought and gained support from a large number of TDs. Ó hÉalaithe went on to say that 'bhí an feachtas ar bhonn náisiúnta ag an phointe sin [1991] agus ar bhonn náisiúnta thosaigh muid ag *lobby*áil na páirtí polaitíochta agus ceann de na rudaí a rinneamar ná an lá *lobby*áil i Buswell's'[31] (Hotel – near the Dáil) ('the campaign was on a national basis at that point [1991], and on a national basis we began to lobby the political parties and one of the things we did was the lobbying day in Buswell's').

Ó Feinneadha explained that they had two meetings in Buswell's Hotel:

> Bhí cruinniú poiblí i Buswell's againn agus bhí cáad duine aige sin. B'shin an chéad cruinniú go bunaíodh an feachtas. Ina dhiaidh san d'ea- graíomar cupla cruinniú le hionadaithe ó na heagraíochtaí agus na pobail Gaeltachta agus Gaeilge éagsúla agus thángamar ar na héilimh a bhí againn agus chuamar ag cur an éileamh sin i láthair na polaiteoirí. Go luath ina dhiaidh sin arís d'eagraíomar lá stocaireachta in Buswell's, mar a thárlaíonn sé, trasna an bóthair ón Dáil. Casamar le leathchéad Teachtaí Dáile an lá sin agus mhíníomar na héilimh a bhí againn. Tógadh pictiúirí le haghaidh páipéirí áitiúla agus fuaireamar geallúintí uathu gur thacaigh siad leis an diabhal rud.[32]

(We had a public meeting in Buswell's and there were a hundred people there. That was the first meeting when the campaign was launched. After that we organised a few meetings with representatives from the various Gaeltacht and Irish-language organisations and communities and we decided on the demands we had and began to present these demands to the politicians. Soon after that again we organised an event to launch the campaign in Buswell's, as it happens, across the road from the Dáil. We met fifty TDs that day and we explained our demands to them. Pictures were taken for local papers and we received promises from them that they would support the damn thing.)

Michael D. Higgins (who later became the Minister responsible for setting up TnaG) had shown his support prior to his appointment as minister. He had attended the two meetings in Buswell's Hotel and a previous meeting in Galway.[33]

---

31 D. Ó hÉalaithe, in a personal interview with the author on 11 April 1997.   32 C. Ó Feinneadha, 1998, op. cit.   33 M.D. Higgins TD, in a personal interview with the author, 4 June 1998.

An emerging consensus

The structure of the Irish-language channel that emerged was in no way inevitable. It emerged early in the process and went relatively unquestioned. However, there was tension within FNT between the Gaeltacht movement for a community-based television channel and the non-Gaeltacht demand for a national channel. Ó Feinneadha explained that 'tríd is tríd ní raibh aon fhadhb againn, cloíomar go docht agus go daingean leis an rud [support for a national channel] agus is Donncha [Ó hÉalaithel an t-aon duine nár chloigh leis sin go hiomlán'[34] ('through and through we had no problem, we adhered to the thing [support for a national channel] strictly and rigidly and Donncha [Ó hÉalaithe] really was the only person who didn't adhere to it completely').

They had reached a consensus from the start, from which Ó hÉalaithe tended to stray, according to Ó Feinneadha. This consensus was that FNT would demand a national Irish-language television channel, as those outside the Gaeltacht wanted, but that it would be 'located and rooted' in the Gaeltacht. However, there had been little opportunity to debate the issue because FNT believed that they required a consensus in order to achieve their aim. However, Ó Gadhra argued that the agenda had already been set by the committee, under the chairmanship of Proinsías Mac Aonghusa, which had produced a document for Haughey in 1991, arguing for a national channel.[35] Ó hÉalaithe agreed that the decision as to whether the Irish-language television channel would be a Gaeltacht television or a national channel had already been decided.[36] Thus, although Ó hÉalaithe backed FNT, he continued to be critical of TnaG and to call for its transformation to a Gaeltacht channel.

It was not until the appointment of Máire Geoghegan-Quinn in 1992 that any action was taken with regard to TnaG. As Haughey's 'successor' (re Irish-language television), Máire Geoghegan-Quinn put TnaG on the agenda for the Department of Communications, met with FNT and hired Pádhraic Ó Ciardha (originally from RTÉ and, later, employed by TnaG from its inception) as her adviser on the matter.

It appears that Geoghegan-Quinn had been interested personally in Irish-language television and had decided to examine the question immediately upon her appointment. Ó Ciardha explained that he was asked, a few days before Easter Sunday 1992, if he would like to be an Irish-language broadcasting adviser and was surprised at being appointed within days. She agreed to meet FNT very soon after she appointed Ó Ciardha as her adviser. It was from this point on that FNT began to gain insider status.

---

34 C. Ó Feinneadha, 1998, op. cit.   **35** N. Ó Gadhra, op. cit.   **36** D. Ó hÉalaithe, op. cit.

Rud spéisiúil faoi Mháire Geoghegan *like* – bhí Feachtas Náisiúnta Teilifíse ag iarraidh cruinniú le fada le Aire Cumarsáide. Nuair a bhí Ray Burke ann níor éirigh lint; nuair a bhí Séamus Brennan ann níor éirigh linn; agus nuair a bhí Máire Geoghegan ann d'éirigh linn.[37]

(An interesting thing about Máire Geoghegan – Feachtas Náisiúnta Teilifíse was requesting a meeting for a long time with a Minister for Communications. When Ray Burke was there we didn't succeed; when Séamus Brennan was there we didn't succeed; and when Máire Geoghegan was there we succeed.)

Ó Ciardha claimed that Geoghegan-Quinn was interested in investigating Irish-language broadcasting and he extolled her uniqueness as a native Irish speaker, a teacher, a parent and a government minister. For Ó Feinneadha and FNT, her appointment was 'a great advancement'.[38] It was with the appointment of Máire Geoghegan-Quinn as Minister for Communications that the political pledges began to be realised. Ó Feinneadha said

An céad *break* a fuaireamar ná go ceapadh Máire Geoghegan-Quinn mar Aire Cumarsáide. Ba léir ón tús go raibh Máire Geoghegan-Quinn tugtha don smaoineamh agus cheap sí Pádhraic Ó Ciardha mar comhairleoir pearsanta aici féin chun dul ag plé leis. Bhuail sí linne agus phléigh sí an rud go mion linn agus ag deireadh an cruinniú bhí *stoney silence* ó ár dtaobh den bhord agus dúramar 'Tá siad ag smaoineamh ar an rud a dheanamh'.[39]

(The first break we got was when Máire Geoghegan-Quinn was appointed Minister for Communications. It was clear from the beginning that Máire Geoghegan-Quinn was committed to the idea and she appointed Pádhraic Ó Ciardha as her own personal adviser to deal with it. She met us and discussed the thing in detail with us and at the end of the meeting there was a stoney silence from our side of the table and we said, 'They're thinking of doing it.')

Ó hÉalaithe claimed that he believed that Geoghegan-Quinn was interested in an Irish-language television channel because she would receive support from her own constituents.[40] However, that may be only one element. Other elements, according to Ó Cíardha, may have been that from her own personal experiences as an Irish speaker from the Gaeltacht, a parent and a teacher she believed there was a need for more Irish-language television

37 D. Ó hÉalaithe, op. cit. **38** C. Ó Feinneadha, 1998, op. cit. **39** Ibid. **40** D. Ó hÉalaithe, op. cit.

programmes.[41] There was a belief expressed by Irish-language organisations that the predominance of English-language television programmes was further undermining the position of the Irish language in the Gaeltacht and that Irish-language television programmes would assist in the preservation and restoration of the Irish language and that Irish citizens had the right to be entertained and informed in Irish. Therefore, Geoghegan-Quinn may have arrived in office predisposed to establishing an Irish-language channel, but she was facilitated by political circumstances – she represented a politically volatile marginal constituency, which included a Gaeltacht region.

Ó Gadhra claimed that when Geoghegan-Quinn left office 'Bhí an rud ar fad beagnach réigh. Níl mé ag iarraidh baint den méid a dhean Michael D'.[42] ('The whole thing was almost ready. I don't want to detract from the amount Michael D. did'). Ó Ciardha also made the same point.[43] However, it must be added that when Geoghegan-Quinn left office the Government had made no firm commitment.

The consensus

Roughly a year later a new coalition emerged and the Programme for Partnership Government negotiated between the Labour Party and the Fianna Fáil Party contained a promise to undertake the establishment of Teilifís na Gaeilge. Responsibility for the establishment of TnaG then rested with the Minister for Arts, Culture and the Gaeltacht, Michael D. Higgins (1993–7). Like Máire Geoghegan-Quinn, Michael D. Higgins represented the Galway West constituency. Representing a constituency which contained a Gaeltacht region added significance to the Teilifís na Gaeilge – Teilifís na Gaeltachta debate. It was under Higgins that TnaG took shape as a national channel based in the Gaeltacht.

It is interesting to note that both Geoghegan-Quinn and Higgins were elected from the same electoral district and that this electoral district includes Connemara (a Gaeltacht region). This constituency has been electorally volatile during the 1980s and 1990s when there were minority governments and unsteady coalitions. One might speculate that while attempting to establish TnaG would pose risks for some politicians, there would be less of a threat to Geoghegan-Quinn's and Higgins' re-election efforts because of the support they might gain from the Gaeltacht region. Particularly considering that TnaG came to be based within that electoral district.

Higgins was (and still is) a sociologist on leave from a lecturing post in the Department of Sociology and Political Science in the National University of Ireland, Galway. According to Ó hÉalaithe, with Higgins' appointment 'Rinne

---

41 P. Ó Ciardha, op. cit.   **42** N. Ó Gadhra, op. cit.   **43** P. Ó Ciardha, op. cit.

sé difríocht an-mhór mar ní fhéadfadh an fear sin an rud a cheilt, bhí sé féin sách fada dhá iarraidh'[44] ('It made a very big difference because that man could not conceal the thing, he had wanted it for so long'). Ó Feinneadha said that FNT thought that Geoghegan-Quinn's efforts had been in vain when she left office 'Ach an rud a thárla *anyway* ná gur ceapadh Michael D. [*laughter*]'[45] ('But the thing that happened anyway was that Michael D. was appointed'). FNT could not believe their good fortune; Michael D. Higgins had attended one of the early meetings of FNT.

Higgins' interest in Irish-language television was clear. As well as attending meetings organised by FNT, he had indicated his interest in the Dáil by raising the issue regularly during Question Time. Ó hÉalaithe said about Higgins:

> *Well*, go bunúsach, an fáth go raibh sé i bhfabhar an teilifís, bhí sé i bhfabhar aon rud a gheobhadh vótaí dó sa nGaeltacht. Bhí sé ag iarraidh é féin a cheangailt isteach le an *progressive dissident element* sa nGaeltacht, mar a déarfá, agus bhí sée ag fáil go leor vótaí i gConamara mar gheall air sin.[46]

> (Well, basically, the reason he was in favour of the television was that he was in favour of anything which would get votes for him in the Gaeltacht. He was trying to tie himself in with the progressive dissident element in the Gaeltacht, as one would say, and he was getting enough votes in Connemara because of that.)

Moreover, Ó hÉalaithe worked for Higgins in his constituency, he also wrote speeches, policy documents and Dáil questions for him and felt that he had a certain influence with Higgins.

Ó hÉalaithe, however, believed that the change in Higgins' objective, from a Gaeltacht television channel to a national channel (from Teilifís na Gaeltachta to Teilifís na Gaeilge), came about when he became minister and was due to the influence of his civil servants. Ó hÉalaithe believed the civil servants had the power to change their Minister's mind. He claimed that Higgins 'Chuaigh sé isteach sa Roinn agus dúradh leis [*by the civil servants*], "You're not giving in to this crowd in the *Geltacht*, this is going to be set up and going to be a national Irish-language television channel"'[47] ('Went into the Department and he was told [*by the civil servants*], "You're not giving in to this crowd in the Gaeltacht, this is going to be set up and going to be a national Irish-language television channel".') Higgins, on the other hand, claimed

44 D. Ó hÉalaithe, op. cit. 45 C. Ó Feinneadha, 1998, op. cit. 46 D. Ó hÉalaithe, op. cit. 47 Ibid.

that it was the civil servants that were influenced by his views, not *vice versa*. Overall, the civil servants gave the impression that they deferred absolutely to the Minister. Even when discussing the problematic relationship with the Department of Finance, they claimed that extracting the finances from the Department of Finance was a matter of sheer political will on the part of the Minister.[48] Moreover, Colm Ó Briain (who was a political adviser to Higgins) claimed that

> the civil servants in the department lined up behind Michael D. against the civil servants in Finance. The problem with dealing with Bertie Ahern [then Minister for Finance and current Taoiseach] was that he was a sort of willow-the-wisp. When he met Michael D. in the corridors he said 'That will be alright, that will be OK' and then the letter that came from Finance was disastrous and sent Michael D. into a tailspin. It did more damage to his health in those two years than any other single act of government.[49]

The civil servants claimed that they would have no personal problems with any decision taken by the Minister. They gave advice to the Minister and accepted the Minister's decision.

However, the civil servants claimed that the previous Minister, Geoghegan-Quinn, took the decision that the new channel would be national rather than Gaeltacht-based. Whether she came to this decision before or after her appointment as Minister for Communications was not known. Perhaps she was influenced in that decision by her adviser Pádhraic Ó Ciardha. Moreover, the civil servants who dealt with broadcasting appear to have confined themselves to the technical issues of frequency allocation. They claimed that support for a national channel was never threatened by support for a Gaeltacht channel, i.e. that a Gaeltacht channel had never been seriously considered by either minister.

Ó hÉalaithe argued that the Gaeltacht position continued to be marginalised, during the first few years of Higgins' term of office. He claimed that the advisory committees appointed by RTÉ and approved by Higgins marginalised the supporters of Teilifís na Gaeltachta. He claimed that

> bhí an taobh Gaeltachta den feachtas ar iarraidh ó thaobh muide i gConamara a bheadh ag argóint go laidir ar son an taobh Gaeltachta den rud – bhí muide gearrtha amach – agus bhí sé sin déanta d'aon ghnó. Cuireadh an rud teicniúil ar bun agus cuireadh mise air sin, ach

---

48 Based on personal interviews with a number of civil servants.   49 C. Ó Briain, in a personal interview with the author on 26 November 1998.

né dóigh liom go gceapfaidís ag an am go raibh an oiread eolas agam faoi chúrsaí teicniúil agus a bhí. Ní dóigh liom go gceapfaidís mé, ach cheap siad gur duine éigin atá ag múineadh matamaitic mé agus atá, b'fhéidir, ag plé leis an nGaeilge agus ní raibh fhios acub go mba innealtóir mé.[50]

(the Gaeltacht side of the campaign was missing in terms of us in Connemara who'd be arguing strongly for the Gaeltacht side of things – we were cut out – and it was done on purpose. The technical committee was set up and I was put on that, but I don't think that they would have known at the time that I had as much knowledge about technical things as I had. I don't think they would have appointed me, but they thought that I was somebody who was teaching mathematics and perhaps dealing with the Irish language and they didn't know I was an engineer.)

As far as Ó hÉalaithe was concerned these committees were set up to control the agenda.

DECIDING THE STRUCTURE OF THE NEW STATION

The establishment of a separate Irish-language channel may have been the result of pressure from FNT or may be due to the interests of the individual ministers (Máire Geoghegan-Quinn and Michael D. Higgins). However, what made the channel acceptable was that the discourse on the Irish language still held an ideological position within national identity in that the majority of the population still favoured Irish-language policies.[51] Irish speakers had been dissatisfied with RTÉ and had given up hope that RTÉ could provide an adequate service within the existing channels. From the perspective of the new national identity, providing a separate Irish-language channel conformed to European Union (EU) principles[52] of decentralisation, enabling communities, diversity, minority rights (also, the structure of the new channel reflected two other principles – supporting small and medium enterprises and cross-border cooperation)[53] and gave the appearance of a modern pluralist state.

Geoghegan-Quinn and Higgins both arrived on the scene prepared to take decisions, to improve the situation of Irish-language television broadcasting

50 D. Ó hÉallaithe, op. cit.   **51** Three quarters (75%) of the population agreed that the government should support the use of Irish on television and three quarters (78%) agreed that the government should support Irish-language organisations (P. Ó Riagáin and M. Ó Gliasáin, op. cit., p. 30).   **52** Cf. European Charter for Regional or Minority Languages.   **53** Independent production companies from Northern Ireland were permitted to, and did, produce programmes for TG4.

and establish a separate television channel. When the Government had taken the decision to allocate money to the TnaG project (in February 1993), Higgins appointed two advisory committees (in April 1993) and then the Government took a decision (on 7 December 1993) to establish TnaG. A few months later RTÉ, with the Minister's consent, announced the appointment of the TnaG Authority, in March 1994. In 1995 Higgins published a discussion paper on broadcasting.[54]

The two committees Higgins established were

> the Coiste Bunaithe and the Coiste Teicniúil, the Coiste Bunaithe was to look at every general aspect, in relation to what I was trying to do, and the Coiste Teicniúil was to get locked into this difficulty of UHF and VHF and others.[55]

Membership of the committees consisted of independent film producers from various Gaeltacht areas and representatives of the social partners, under the chairmanship of Gearóid Ó Tuathaigh from the National University of Ireland, Galway. Higgins placed representatives from FNT on both committees. Feargal Mac Amhlaoibh, FNT's chairman, and Ciarán Ó Feinneadha, FNT's treasurer, were both on the Coiste Bunaithe. Donncha Ó hÉalaithe, FNT's public relations officer, was on the Coiste Teicniuil.

These committees made recommendations for the Minister to consider. The Coiste Bunaithe advised that the channel broadcast three hours a day – one hour from RTÉ, one from independent producers in the Gaeltacht and one from abroad (to be dubbed or subtitled). They advised that not more than 40% of the material be dubbed or subtitled; that at least 30% of broadcast time be aimed at children under twelve with an emphasis on teenagers as well; that RTÉ be responsible for building the broadcasting base and employing staff and allow TnaG to use its regional studios; that the channel be used for distance education, foreign-language material and Oireachtas coverage; and that it have a teletext service from the outset. Furthermore, it was suggested that the headquarters be sited in the Gaeltacht (like Raidió na Gaeltachta). Many, but not all, of the suggestions were taken on board.

In relation to the Coiste Teicniúil Ó hÉalaithe claimed

> bhí sé suimiúil dhomsa, *anyways*, ar an gCoiste Teicniúil. *RTÉ were in there, were controlling, were running with this nov* chun a chinntiú go dtárlódh sé sa mbealach is lú a ndéanfadh sé dochar do RTÉ. Ba é sin an cuid den *agenda* a bhí acub – 'Cad é an bealach is lú a dhéanadh sé

54 Department of Arts, Culture and the Gaeltacht, op. cit.   **55** M.D. Higgins TD, op. cit.

dochar dhúinn.' Cinote tá mé céad faoin gcéad cinate de sin anois th'éis an méid atá ag tárlú.[56]

(It was interesting for me anyways on the Coiste Teicniúil. RTÉ were in there, were controlling, were running with this now to ensure that it happened in the way that would cause the least harm to RTÉ. That was the part of the agenda they had – 'What is the way that it would cause the least harm to us?' Certainly, I am one hundred per cent certain of that now after all that's happening.)

On 24 January 1994 Higgins announced that RTÉ would establish a TnaG Authority within a week or two. After considerable delay the Authority was announced on 11 March 1994. Ó Feinneadha from FNT was appointed to the Authority. FNT had become increasingly inactive the more certain they were that TnaG would come into existence. Ó Feinneadha made the point that he represented FNT on the TnaG Authority:

bhíos-sa ann agus ainm orm fhéin mar duine a bhí ann thar ceann an Fheachtais. *Now*, agus sin ráite agam, rinne an Feachtas soiléir é go raibh siad ag stopadh ag feidhmiú ag an pointe sin mar go raibh agóid láidir déanta. Níor oibrigh an Feachtas ach b'fhéidir uair amháin sa tréimhse iar-chomhairle TnaG mar thuigeamar dá mba rud é go raith dhá dream ag iarraidh an rud céanna a bhrú chun cinn go bhféadfaí praiseach iomlán a dhéanamh den rud. Tar éis go ndearna an Rialtas cinneadh go raibh siad chun TnaG a bhunú, d'imigh an rud ó bheith ina éileamh ón bpobal go dtí polasaí an rialtais. Ba mhór an t-athrú a rinne sé sin ar an saol. Ní *outsiders* a bhí ionainn a thuilleadh – ba *insiders* muid.[57]

(I was there with the name of being somebody who was there representing the Feachtas. Now, having said that, the Feachtas made it clear that they were stopping operating at that point because a strong protest had been made. The Feachtas didn't work except maybe once in the post-TnaG-Authority era because we understood that if two groups wanted to push the same thing forward a complete mess could be made of the thing. After the Government took the decision that they were going to establish TnaG, the thing went from being a demand from the community to a government policy. It made a big difference to life. We weren't outsiders anymore – we were insiders.)

56 D. Ó hÉalaithe, op. cit.   **57** C. Ó Feinneadha, 1998, op. cit.

FNT gradually disbanded so that by the time Ó hÉalaithe was appointed to the TnaG Authority in 1997, FNT no longer existed. Ó hÉalaithe returned firmly to his original position of demanding a Gaeltacht television service and made regular criticisms of TnaG.

GOVERNMENT OPPOSITION TO THE NEW STATION

Higgins' success appeared to have depended on the principles underlying his policies (such as broadcasting diversity or citizenship rights). He said:

> I always stressed that I was taking a decision from the principle of broadcasting diversity and citizenship rights rather than a revivalist strategy. Yes, it would help, of course, the use of Irish and whatever, but that wasn't the primary purpose; my purpose was very much in relation to the form of indigenous culture, of establishing certain kinds of principles of sovereignty in relation to culture, but also more importantly was contributing to diversity.[58]

Having principles on which he could build helped guide him in a clear direction, it also reinforced his tenacity. His principles were also ideologically acceptable in the era since the redefinition of identity in the 1960s and 1970s and the further ideological shift during the 1980s and 1990s. He was resolute in his efforts and was unwilling to be moved on certain issues. As he said himself:

> And there came one or two points in it, where I regarded two or three items as fundamental items. If I had been defeated in Cabinet on the Order under Section 31, I would probably have resigned.[59]

He appeared to have been willing to risk his political position to remove the censorship under Section 31, although perhaps he was not willing to take the same risk for the sake of TnaG.

Furthermore, he was articulate, although he found it difficult to employ theoretical language in the 'practical' work of a minister. He claimed that 'the *Independent* mocked every time I tried to offer a concept like the "communicative space" – it was horrific'.[60] As Minister he had attempted to articulate theoretical concepts in a policy environment. Moreover, Ó hÉalaithe claimed that Higgins 'ag deanamh speechanna míle uair níos fearr ná mar a fhéadfainn

---

58 M.D. Higgins TD, op. cit.   **59** Ibid.   **60** Ibid.

é a dhéanamh mar gheall ar go raibh sé i ndán tarraingt as an saghas back-ground socheolaíochta a bhí aige agus bhí sé iontach'[61] ('made speeches a thousand times better than I could because he could draw on the kind of soci-ological background he had and it was wonderful').

He also must have been able to convince his cabinet colleagues. Whether or not Higgins carried weight at the cabinet table is unanswered because of the secrecy or confidentiality surrounding such meetings. However, one could speculate that he carried some weight, judging from his achievements. As well as the Government's decision to establish TnaG, Higgins was behind the deci-sion to remove both the 'cap' (limit) which had been imposed on RTÉ's adver-tising revenue and Section 31 (censorship of proscribed organisations and those associated with them, such as Sinn Féin).[62]

Moreover, O Briain claimed that 'Máire Geoghegan-Quinn was very important to Michael D. in taking the temperature in Fianna Fáil'.[63] Higgins had an ally in the other government party and at the cabinet table. Geoghegan-Quinn maintained her support for the project she had initiated. One would presume that as a minister she supported Higgins at the cabinet table when they discussed TnaG.

The Minister's role in producing TnaG was not as straightforward as might be imagined from the discussion thus far. The relationship between Higgins and the Department of Finance does not appear to have been lacking in acrimony. For example, RTÉ had earned IR£16 million (€20,316,000) more from advertising than it had been permitted while the 'cap' was in place. Higgins claimed this money. However, he argued that

> An indicator of the row and battle I had to have was that the Department of Finance insisted on I surrendering some of that money, but I kept four point five million of that.[64]

Furthermore, Ó Briain claimed that

> invariably when he [Higgins] brought proposals to Cabinet the Minister for Finance, who was Bertie Ahern, sought opposing docu-ments, even when Michael D. got the decision in Cabinet. I don't know if he spoke to you about officials in the Department of Finance subvert-ing the Constitution. They made life hell for him. Most other Ministers have a problem because they don't have the money. He had

61 D. Ó hÉalaithe, op. cit.   **62** This was related to the violence in Northern Ireland. Higgins refused the Taoiseach's efforts to link its removal to negotiations in Northern Ireland because Higgins felt it was a censorship issue and nothing more. Nonetheless, the Taoiseach, Albert Reynolds, claimed publicly, on a number of occasions, that he (Reynolds) had abolished Section 31 as part of the Northern 'peace process'.   **63** C. Ó Briain, op. cit.   **64** M.D. Higgins TD, op. cit.

the money and it was earmarked and Finance raided it and took thirteen million off him, back into the exchequer and all of it was to undermine and to make it less feasible for him to advance.[65]

As well as battling over the money, Higgins and the Department of Finance argued over the interpretation of legislation with regard to spending this money. It seems that even if issues have been discussed repeatedly over a long period of time by officials from two Departments, there can be confrontations between spending ministers and the Department of Finance. Higgins pointed out that 'there was one very angry meeting at which I said to them that if they had been in any way realistic about the Irish language I wouldn't need to be establishing a station'.[66]

PUBLIC REACTION TO THE PROPOSED STATION

While Geoghegan-Quinn had entered office with a certain predisposition toward Irish-language broadcasting, she appeared to be willing to consider proposals and therefore appointed an adviser to investigate the matter of Irish-language broadcasting generally. Higgins, on the other hand, appeared to be committed to a separate Irish-language television channel. He entered office 'knowing what had to be done'. However, Higgins was fully aware of political manoeuvrings. At one stage he held a meeting with an official from Bord na Gaeilge[67] who, with a number of others, undertook 'to ring the Irish-language organisations because I was very vulnerable several times in Cabinet on it because the *Independent* campaign nearly succeeded. It wasn't affecting me, it was dislodging some of my Cabinet colleagues'.[68] The *Irish Independent* appeared to have had a campaign against TnaG, publishing headlines such as 'Use TV Millions For Health Service'.[69]

Higgins was well aware of the political risks and attempted to form some defence. Moreover, Higgins' (and Geoghegan-Quinn's) adviser, Pádhraic Ó Ciardha, was also cognizant of the political environment. He claimed that some politicians were in favour of TnaG, some were against and others didn't care and 'Mar sin is ionramháil pholaitiúl le "p" beag, mar a deirim, lucht an ainchreidimh a thabhairt ar a gcreideamh agus lucht an chreidimh láidir a chur ag obair orthu sin a bhí ar bheagán chreidimh'[70] ('Therefore it was a political, with a small "p", manoeuvre, as I say, to convert the unbelievers and get the firm believers working on those of little faith'). Furthermore, providing a deeper insight into the public sphere in Ireland, O Ciardha said

65 C. Ó Briain, op. cit. 66 M.D. Higgins TD, op. cit. 67 Bord na Gaeilge is an Irish-language state body. 68 Ibid. 69 *Irish Independent* (6 December 1993), p. 19. 70 P. Ó Ciardha, op. cit.

Seo í Éire agus cuireann daoine aithne ar a chéile agus an té a bhfuil taithí aige mar iriseoir [Ó Ciardha had been a journalist in RTÉ] agus a chuireann suim i gcúrsaí polaitíochta bíonn sé ar an eolas faoi céard iad na *foibles* éagsúla atá ag na hairí agus cé na dáilcheantair atá acu ó thaobh na tíreolaíochta de agus ó thaobh sainspéiseanna. Is tír bheag í agus is tír iontach í agus tá an t-ádh orainn go bhfuil polaiteoirí againn a bhfuil suimeanna éagsúla acub agus go bhfuil saol acub taobh amuigh den pholaitíocht. Agus má tá aire agat – agus bhí – ar sulm leo cúrsaí spóirt nó cúrsaí talmhaíochta nó pé rud é taobh amuigh dá *portfolio* oifigiúil, tig leat oibriú ar sin.[71]

(This is Ireland and people get to know one another and somebody who has experience as a journalist [Ó Ciardha had been a journalist in RTÉ] and has an interest in politics knows the different foibles of the ministers and which electoral districts are theirs in terms of geography and in terms of particular interests. It is a small country and it is a wonderful country and we are lucky to have politicians with different interests and a life outside politics. And if there is a minister – and there was – interested in sports or agriculture or whatever outside their official portfolio, you can work on that).

Ó Ciardha appeared to play a very active role an indirect consequence of which was countering some of the political risks the Minister might face with regard to TnaG. Although Ó Feinneadha claimed that FNT had no interest in protecting Higgins they were only interested in protecting TnaG,[72] they also indirectly eliminated some of the risks posed by the media for Higgins.

Figure 5.1: Programmes in Irish and in total on television, 1965–99[73]

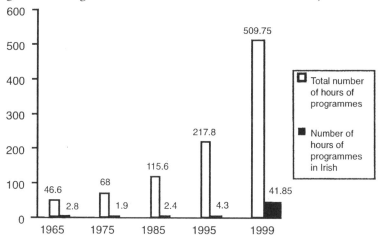

71 Ibid.   **72** C. Ó Feinneadha, 1998, op. cit.   **73** This figure is based on the data in Tables 3.1, 4.1, 4.2 and 5.1.

There was some small amount of debate about TnaG at the stage when it was virtually a *fait accompli*, for example, there were fourteen letters to the editor relating to TnaG in the *Irish Times* during the last two months of 1993: six supporting it and eight opposing it. The addresses of the writers were clearly divided between support in the Gaeltacht areas and opposition especially in the urban middle class, but also from wealthy farmers. This, of course, is a generalisation and is an unproven hypothesis. However, the arguments in support of TnaG were mostly replies to criticisms and also claims that TnaG is necessary for the survival of the Irish language and for raising children in the Gaeltacht, and that Irish speakers have a right to their own television channel. The objections were usually criticisms of the cost while also often supporting the Irish language in theory. Moreover, the words used in these criticisms were often emotive.

There were a few positive signs of support for TnaG, for example, a tele-poll on the *Gay Byrne* (radio) *Show* which had a result of 60% in favour of TnaG, the *Evening Echo* poll which had the result of 80% in favour, and there was a debate in the Dublin County Council in which twenty-three out of thirty-three councillors voted not to complain about the cost of TnaG.

Most of the arguments in favour of the establishment of the separate Irish-language channel were premised on a minority-rights philosophy. Both the Fianna Fáil-Labour coalition[74] and the Fine Gael-Labour-Democratic Left coalition[75] presented TnaG as a service through Irish for the Irish-speaking and Gaeltacht community. TnaG also accepted this viewpoint in its response to the 1995 Green Paper on Broadcasting[76] and in its apologetic *Cén Fáth TnaG?* (Why TnaG?)[77] argued that the Irish-language community has a right to a comprehensive television service in their own language.

The headquarters of TnaG was built in Geoghan-Quinn's and Higgins' constituency and provided jobs both directly in the headquarters and indirectly in independent-production companies. In September 1993 it was believed that the headquarters would be based in the Connemara Gaeltacht. In October Údarás na Gaeltachta asked permission to build the studio in An Spidéal (in Connemara). Meanwhile local groups and local politicians were pressing for the headquarters to be based in their localities in various parts of

74 Fianna Fáil and the Labour Party, *Programme for partnership government 1993–1997: fostering our language, culture and heritage: expanding bilingualism in Irish society: guidelines for action programmes in the State sector* (Fianna Fáil and the Labour Party, 1993), p. 5.   **75** Fine Gael, the Labour Party and Democratic Left, *A Government of renewal: a policy agreement between Fine Gael, the Labour Party and Democratic Left* (Fine Gael, the Labour Party and Democratic Left, 1994), p. 84.   **76** TnaG's unpublished response to the Green Paper on Broadcasting, op. cit., p. 12.   **77** TnaG, *Cén Fáth TnaG* (Dublin: TnaG, 1995).

the Connemara Gaeltacht, some of the suggested areas were: Ros Muc, Casla, Baile na hAbhann and An Spidéal. But eventually it was decided to build the headquarters in Baile na hAbhann (in Connemara).

One of the benefits promoted by the Minister (Michael D. Higgins) was the employment potential. Originally the Minister claimed that the new channel would create two hundred and fifty jobs directly, later he added that a total of six hundred would be created because of the indirect influence on independent producers, finally he said that more than two hundred jobs would be created.

The major bone of contention for the public at large and the only issue which seemed to spark any debate was the cost of setting up and running TnaG. The Working Group had said that the capital costs would be over IR£8 million (€10,158,000) and the annual costs would be IR£15 million.[78] But when the situation was seriously considered it was decided that the capital costs of setting up the channel would be IR£15 million. However, by October or November 1993 this had risen to IR£17,350,000 (€22.03 million) capital costs and the annual running cost had risen to IR£21. The running costs are lower for TnaG because RTÉ is obliged to provide some programmes and other services and resources free of charge, reducing the running cost to IR£16 million (€20.315 million) per annum.

Where the money would come from was the main source of contention here. From the beginning the Coiste Bunaithe had wanted to dissociate itself from any increase in the licence fee and therefore was seriously considering a few other sources of funding, namely the EU, the National Lottery and the raising of RTÉ's advertising 'cap' could provide some funding. The amount that RTÉ earned in excess of the cap between 1990 and 1993 provided the necessary capital for building the broadcasting base. The *Irish Independent* on a number of occasions claimed that the new service would be paid for from an increase in the licence fee and from a tax on video rental. This caused controversy among the general public and especially vociferous in their complaints were the Video Retailers' Association and Xtra Vision, towards the end of November 1993. The Minister, the Coiste Bunaithe and various of their spokesmen claimed that there would be no increase in the licence fee and there would be no tax on video rental aimed at funding TnaG. There was an increase in the television licence fee, however, from sixty-two to seventy punts within a year of TnaG coming on the air and this extra eight punts per licence amounted to IR£5 million (€6,349,000), which, according to Horgan, 'was almost exactly equal to the (revised) cost of the subsidy which RTÉ was now required to give to the Gaeltacht station [*sic*]'.[79]

---

78 Working Group on Irish Language Broadcasting, op. cit.   **79** J. Horgan, op. cit. p. 184. Horgan appears to be unaware of the tension between the Gaeltacht and national campaign for TnaG and misnamed the channel Teilifís na Gaeltachta.

The reasons for placing the headquarters in the Gaeltacht are varied, but the particular Gaeltacht in which it was built is within Geoghan-Quinn's and Higgins' constituency and is believed to be one of the 'stronger' Gaeltachts. An important reason for basing TnaG in a Gaeltacht is to facilitate the use of Irish as the working language of the station. Although, from the start the working language was to be Irish, in February 1994 an advertisement in English was placed in the national newspapers for an engineer for TnaG and there was no mention of the need to be able to speak Irish. There have also been several complaints that English was being spoken by TnaG staff. Ó hÉalaithe said:

> Caithfidh go mbeidh tuiscint ag an dream atá ag déanamh na cláracha ar an teanga atá dhá úsáaid. Is mór an náire an Nuacht TnG [*sic*] mar gheall ar níl Gaeilge ag an gcriú teilifíse a théann amach. Tá muid ag caint ar teanga atá faoi bhrú agus, i gcás na Gaeltachta, teanga ar mionlach an-bheag iad a bhfuil, saghas, a cuid *self-esteem* an-íseal. Má théann tú isteach sa phobal sin agus, saghas, 'muide lucht na teilifíse ag teacht le agallamh a dhéanamh leatsa i do theanga, ach níl mnid chun do theanga a usáid'. Tá mé th'éis diúltú agallamh a dhéanamh le Nuacht TnG. Dúirt mé, 'Caithfidh sibh criú Gaeilge a chur chúm.[80]

> (People making programmes must understand the language being used. It is shameful that TnG [*sic*] News sends out crews that don't speak Irish. We're talking about a language under pressure and, in the case of the Gaeltacht, a minority language and a community with low self-esteem. They go into that community as the 'TV people' coming to interview you in your language, but they won't use your language when talking to each other. I've refused to do an interview with TnG News. I said you have to send me a crew with Irish.)

Throughout this three-year period from the Government's decision, at the end of 1993, to build TnaG, until its launch in the autumn of 1996 there was a mixture of hope and trepidation. As part of the evolving plan for the birth of TnaG, there were almost weekly announcements of delays and changes. For example, the biggest delay involved the commencement of broadcasting. In October 1993 the Coiste Bunaithe advised that broadcasting should commence by the end of 1994. But by the beginning of November 1993 there was scepticism amongst Irish-language groups and some felt that it would be the end of 1996, if ever. However, after a Cabinet decision at the end of November 1993 it was claimed that the channel would begin broadcasting by

80 D. Ó hÉalaithe, op. cit.

January 1995 (the broadcasting network would only be able to reach 60% of the population at that stage). Then at the beginning of December 1993 it was mentioned that 90% of the population would be reached by mid-1996 and 98% by mid-1997. By March 1994 the start-up date was estimated at the end of 1995 and broadcasts should reach 90% of the population from the start. In February 1994 FNT expressed their fears that it would be 1996 before broadcasting could commence, but Robert Gahan from RTÉ said that the estimated date was still the end of 1995. However, TnaG began broadcasting on 31 October 1996. Legally TnaG is part of RTÉ, however, currently the relationship between RTÉ and TnaG is permitted to change under the Broadcasting Act 2001.

TnaG emerged from a unique situation, a convergence of forces. It can be explained partly by the ideologies which had produced the discourses on preservation, restoration and rights. This is the soil from which Irish broadcasting grew; this is the context within which the Gaeltacht civil rights movement operated; this is the background for understanding the Gaeltacht groups of the 1980s and FNT. Geoghegan-Quinn and Higgins were more closely associated with all this through the Connemara Gaeltacht, a factor which was missing for the previous ministers – Charles Haughey, Ray Burke and Seamus Brennan. However, Haughey was from an earlier generation which had closer ties with the national(ist) ideology of nation-building, nonetheless, this was not sufficient to overcome the 'political reality' of a career politician or the fiscal rectitude of the late 1980s.

---

3 Cf. J.B. Thompson, 'Ideology and modern culture' in A. Giddens, D. Held, D. Hubert, D. Seymore and J. Thompson (eds), *The polity reader in social theory* (Cambridge : Polity Press, 1994), particularly p. 135 for a discussion of a more critical, as opposed to passive, conceptualisation of ideology.

CHAPTER 6

The birth of a station

The main context in which TnaG emerged was the shift from a more liberal to a more neoliberal ideology, from a more European to a more global environment. At the heart of this was an increasing emphasis on the democratic principles of citizenship such as freedom of choice and access to the public sphere. These principles, as well as the contradictions contained within them, are reflected in TnaG. The main contradiction, which existed in the liberal ideology, is that although minorities have rights, they must be self-supporting.

A further contradiction which emerged is that citizenship, as a universal concept, does not take into account the diversity of people and their experiences. This has particular consequences for minorities, such as Irish speakers. Paradoxically, at the heart of citizenship is the ideal that a diversity of people can co-exist as citizens of the same nation. This is the main reason why advocates of the modern ideology emphasised democracy and citizenship and individualised identity. Discussing the term 'nation', Habermas argued that in classical usage it referred to communities of people with the same descent, with a common language, customs and traditions.[1] This classical usage regards the nation as pre-political. With the formation of nation states, however, the pre-political homogeneous membership ideally becomes a 'nation of citizens [which] does not derive its identity from some common ethnic and cultural properties, but rather from the *praxis* of citizens who actively exercise their civil rights'.[2]

Furthermore, Habermas argued that political culture

> by no means has to be based on all citizens sharing the same language or the same ethnic and cultural origins. Rather, the political culture must serve as the common denominator for a constitutional patriotism which simultaneously sharpens an awareness of the multiplicity and integrity of the different forms of life which coexist in a multicultural society.[3]

1 J. Habermas, 'Citizenship and national identity: some reflections on the future of Europe', *Praxis International* 12(1), 1992, p. 3.   2 Ibid.   3 J. Habermas, 1992, op.cit. p. 7.

The individual as a citizen is, therefore, a member of a political culture. It is this common political culture which binds all citizens together. Thus, all the citizens of one 'nation' are loyal to one political culture while also having the freedom to play other roles and have disparate loyalties, identities, cultures, languages, etc.

A number of authors (such as Iris Young),[4] however, have argued that citizenship actually promotes what people have in common and disregards differences. Similarly, Harrison contended that it is the differences between people that result in their having different experiences of citizenship.[5]

Irish speakers, while a national minority in a global context, have the advantage of possessing one of the 'props' of Irish national identity. Therefore, Irish speakers are bound into the national culture. Their use of the Irish language, however, simultaneously integrates them into Irish culture and alienates them from civil society and the political culture which is predominantly in the English language. Habermas, although he mentioned language, appears to overlook the problem that all different linguistic groups in a multicultural society cannot use their different languages in one national political culture (civil society and public sphere, including the mass media) simultaneously.[6]

The notion of differential rights combined with the consumerisation of citizenship has made Turner's 'cultural citizenship'[7] appear to be a legitimate aspect of citizenship. Part of the social rights of Irish speakers is to participate in their own culture, the unique feature of which is speaking Irish. In this context the emergence of TnaG may be perceived as an element of citizenship rather than purely consumerist. Consuming Irish-language programmes, according to this argument, is an element of participation in cultural citizenship even if it is a culture-consuming, rather than a culture-debating, public. In this light the provision of Irish-language 'products' is a social right. This is an argument made by Irish-language organisations, and acceptable within the neoliberal ideology.

THE FIRST IRISH-LANGUAGE TELEVISION STATION BEGINS

TnaG began broadcasting on Hallowe'en (31 October) 1996. The channel began with great publicity and the promotion of its logo 'súil eile' ('another eye', or 'another perspective'). It was clear that TnaG was trying to find a

4 I.M. Young, 'Polity and group difference: a critique of the ideal of universal citizenship', *Ethics* (99), 1989.   5 M.L. Harrison, 'Citizenship, consumption and rights: a comment on B.S. Turner's theory of citizenship', *Sociology* 25:2 (1991).   6 J. Habermas, 1992, op. cit.   7 B.S. Turner, op. cit. and B.S. Turner, 'Further specification of the citizenship concept: a reply to M.L. Harrison', *Sociology* 25:2 (1991).

niche for itself as an alternative to the other television channels by providing another perspective. It tried to emphasise the different view of the world that TnaG would provide, but not the difference in language. Although established as a minority channel, TnaG tried to maximise its audience to include people with little or no Irish as well as Irish speakers, mainly because of the practice of broadcasting and the rational nature of the market (echoing recent ideologies) and to a lesser degree to reflect the discourse on the Irish language (restoration of Irish according to the earlier ideology). Ó Ciardha made it clear that the channel would not focus on serving only Irish speakers. He claimed that the *raison d'être* of the channel was to provide a new television service for the Irish public as a whole and that it just happened to be in Irish.[8] He went on to argue that neither did they intend to provide an Irish-language version of RTÉ, nor did they regard themselves as an instrument of the Government's language policy.[9] TnaG is subject to the same considerations as RTÉ, as a national rather than a minority or community channel, to try to attract a large audience, and it broadcasts programmes in Irish and English to appeal to Irish speakers and non-Irish speakers.

Viewers: cost and programmes

A few years before TnaG came on air Frank Fitzgibbon in the *Sunday Tribune* complained about its potential audience figures, claiming that on RTÉ the Nuacht has a viewership of only 114,000 while the main evening News commands an audience of 600,000. He also compared (the Irish-language current affairs programme) *Cúrsaí*'s viewership with that of *Tuesday File* and *Prime Time*, claiming that the difference was 75,000 as opposed to 350,000.[10] However, the comparison is disingenuous; taking the percentage of Irish speakers in Ireland to be about 10% one would expect Irish language programmes to achieve about 10% of their English language equivalents. In fact, in both these comparisons the Irish language programmes achieved audiences of about 20% of their English language counterparts, thus suggesting that they are twice as successful, given their relative potential audience. Nonetheless, absolute numbers, and not relative numbers, attract advertising revenue. Fitzgibbon also claimed that if the Government was to pay for TnaG by licence fee only it would add an extra £25 to £30 to the fee and asked the rhetorical question 'What would we all feel about that?',[11] even though he knew that the increase discussed was between £5 and £10 and that the Coiste Bunaithe wanted no increase for fear of opposition.

8 Similarly Seosamh Ó Tuairisc said to Hourigan in an interview that RnaG was a local radio station that just happened to be in Irish because the people spoke Irish (Hourigan, 2001, op. cit., p. 28). **9** P. Ó Ciardha, in a personal interview with the author on 19 February 1996. **10** *Sunday Tribune* (5 December 1993), p. 2. **11** Ibid.

Achieving success within the market involves enticing an audience. This means providing programmes which are attractive. The primary principle of attractive programming is quality and a principal requirement for achieving quality is finance. The Minister for Arts, Culture and the Gaeltacht required RTÉ to provide one hour per day of programming to TnaG at a cost of *circa* £5 million (€6,349,000).[12] This expenditure was equal to an average of over IR£13,500 per hour – RTÉ's average expenditure on independent productions was over £20,000 per hour (in the UK, ITV spent about six times as much). TnaG was provided with £10 million per annum from the exchequer (this increased to £13 million a few years later and to €28,800,000 in 2001), from which TnaG provided two hours per day, which averaged at £13,500 (€17,141) per hour. However, through a policy of repeats (i.e. providing an average of only one 'original' hour per day) TnaG claimed that its average expenditure on commissioning programmes was similar to RTÉ's at around £20,000 per hour. Ó Ciardha argued that although the Welsh station, S4C, has a budget at least seven times as big as TnaG's, TnaG would be able to bring its average expenditure per hour on production up to RTÉ's level.[13]

TnaG has also had the option of supplementing its finances through selling air-time outside its main schedule and through advertising within the schedule. Achieving the maximum finances from advertising requires maximising the audience. (One example was the programme *Olé Olé* which showed highlights of Spanish and Scottish soccer.) TnaG realises that it is subject to market forces. Ó Ciardha made this point clearly when he claimed that the size of the audience would not matter if TnaG could attract a small audience with a large expendable income.[14]

In broadcasting it is necessary to have some idea of who is watching in order to know what types of programme to broadcast. TnaG carried out market research to provide a clearer picture of the audience, and claimed that the six- to fourteen-year-old audience was central (with programmes such as *Gearóid na Gaisce* (Inspector Gadget) and *Kúigear Kangaroo* (a cartoon about five kangaroos)). This seems to be a manifestation of the policy of preserving the language through concentrating on young people (as most Irish-language organisations do) rather than simply providing an Irish-language television service.

Overall, the aim seems primarily to support the earlier ideology – attempting to preserve the language by concentrating on young people and appeal to the whole nation – even people with a little (or no) Irish – in an attempt to increase the number of Irish speakers. This is clear in its *Cén Fáth*

---

12 RTÉ maintains that in 2001 this cost it €7,500,000. **13** P. Ó Ciardha, 1996, op. cit. **14** Ibid.

TnaG[15] where it claims that it is a cause of disappointment for a lot of people that they didn't manage to master the language when they were at school and that TnaG would give them the chance to have the second opportunity to learn the Irish language.

With regard to the schedule, TnaG initially said it would focus its broadcasting on the period 12.30–2 p.m. for young children, 5–6 p.m. for older children, and 8–10 p.m. for adults, with an emphasis on young people aged fourteen to mid-thirties[16] and use the other times (i.e. mid-afternoon as well as early and late evening) for programmes in English. However, it has tended to expand on that shorter schedule and integrate the programmes in English with the programmes in Irish.

In the early years of RTÉ there was an attempt to include the Irish language throughout the schedule in an attempt to compel the nation to hear some Irish (the 'diffusion policy').[17] This was still evident during the mid 1990s (e.g. during the 1995 Divorce Referendum count and the policy of the Head of Irish Language Programming in RTÉ, Neasa Ní Chinnéide). The types of Irish-language programmes that have been broadcast, however, have been informational and therefore cheaper, but less attractive to non-Irish speakers and, consequently, aimed at Irish speakers as a minority interest. Barbara O'Connor argued that 'drama has an advantage over actuality material in a situation where many people have some knowledge of Irish in that understanding is facilitated by the dramatic action, whereas in current affairs etc., people are solely dependent on linguistic ability'.[18] TnaG has emphasised drama with comedy series such as *C.U. Burn* (a facetious title for a black comedy about a crematorium) and *Gleann Ceo* (a similar comedy revolving around a policeman in a village), and a soap opera called *Ros na Rún* (set in the fictional village of Ros na Rún). *Ros na Rún* was commissioned from independent producers EO Teilifís and Tyrone Productions at a cost of £2.5 million (€3,174,345)[19] or 25% of TnaG's annual budget, suggesting that it was a centrepiece on the new channel. Cathal Goan (Head of TnaG until March 2000 when he became Director of Television at RTÉ) claimed that *Ros na Rún* would be the anchor in the schedule.[20]

Ros na Rún began with two half-hour slots a week with an omnibus edition on Saturdays (each episode and the omnibus were repeated the following day) and increased to four half-hour slots a week. *Ros na Rún* had been piloted on RTÉ at Christmas 1992 and purported to have been amongst the top ten

---

15 TnaG, op. cit. 16 J. Gogan, op. cit, p. 15 and the *Irish Times* (17 April 1996). 17 L. Doolan et al., op. cit., p. 292. 18 B. O'Connor, op. cit., p. 10. 19 Interview with Cathal Goan in the *Irish Times* (17 April 1996). 20 Ibid.

Figure 6.1: Average number of viewers of *Ros na Rún* and other soap operas on RTE1 and Network2 (28 Dec. 1992–3 Jan. 1993).[21]

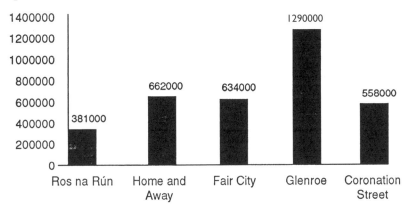

highest rated programmes in the country[22] and it compared favourably with even the most popular, well-established English language soap operas on RTÉ at the time (see Figure 6.1) and was expected to achieve high ratings on TnaG as well. There was evidence of a successful minority-language soap opera in Scotland as well. The Gaelic soap opera *Machair* had up to 500,000 viewers,[23] even though there were only around 50,000 Gaelic speakers. It was hoped that *Ros na Rún* would attract viewers with varying abilities of Irish from fluency to *cúpla focail* (a few words). TnaG has subtitles in English available on teletext; this means that the programmes are accessible to people with little or no Irish, thus widening the potential audience. *Ros na Rún* was not as successful on TnaG as it had been on RTÉ. The advantage that *Ros na Rún* had on RTÉ (and that *Machair* had in Scotland) was that it was broadcast on a channel that is the first or one of the first on the 'dial' – in general the average audience decreases the further the channel is down the 'dial'.

Overall, TnaG's audience is regarded as including all Irish people within the whole island ('an comhthéacs uile Éireannach',[24] 'The all-Ireland context') and beyond ('go ndéanfaimis cúram den phobal líonmhar sin de bhunú agus de dúchas na hÉireann atá ina gcónaí thar sáile',[25] 'that we care for that large community of Irish descent who are living abroad') within a European perspective.[26] The aim, therefore, does not seem to be to serve the minority Irish-speaking community, as TnaG has attempted to amass a large audience irrespective of their ability to speak Irish. Although achieving a large audience

21 This figure is based on data received from RTÉ by the author.   **22** This was reported on the television programme *Market Place* on 6 March 1996, however, *Ros na Rún* was not in the 'Top Twenty' which was published in *RTÉ Guide*.   **23** *Irish Times* (3 November 1993).   **24** From TnaG's unpublished response to the Green Paper on Broadcasting, op. cit, p. 3.   **25** Ibid., p. 15.   **26** From TnaG's polemical 'Why TnaG?', op. cit.

helps construct the national narrative, it seems that the force behind the decision to attract a large audience is the market – survival depends on attracting
a large enough audience to provide some degree of financial viability through
advertising. TnaG's aim was to receive £2 million (€2,540,000) in advertising
revenue during its first year of broadcasting.[27]

Attracting a large audience is a survival tactic. Although TnaG emphasised
that it was an alternative channel rather than 'just' an Irish-language channel,
the channel secures a very strong Gaeltacht quality from its presenters and
actors, its news and current affairs coverage, as well as from many of the entertainment programmes.

Making the programmes

With regard to the production of programmes, TnaG is a 'publisher'. This is
different from the 'production model' used by RTÉ to produce programmes,
which has been predominantly 'fordist'.[28] Tunstall called it the 'integrated
factory'[29] approach, in which programmes are produced internally.[30] In recent
years pressure has been mounting for increased home production on RTÉ,
especially within the 'publisher' approach (i.e. commissioning programmes
from independent producers). Channel 4 and ITV have operated according
to the publisher model, while BBC and RTÉ have been moving towards this
model. TnaG has not produced any of its own programmes, it has commissioned programmes from independent producers, it has also received one
hour per day from RTÉ (including news), some of which may be independently produced. This approach is more post-fordist and is believed to be
more flexible, more efficient, smaller and to increase creativity. According to
Robbins and Cornford, 'the rise of independent production has seemed to be
not only desirable, but also to reflect the post-fordist way the world was
going anyway. A powerful economic and cultural logic is apparently at
work'.[31] However, the creative autonomy of the independent producers is
limited; they produce what the broadcaster demands. As Ó Ciardha argued,
it is an open market in which some particular companies prefer to focus on
specific elements. He claimed that there was a company in the south which

---

27 *Irish Times* (28 April 1996). TnaG did not achieve this, and only reached half that amount a few years
later.   **28** Fordism, simply put, is assembly-line production. Fordism suggests large-scale, slow, struc-
tured, inefficient and inflexible. The commissioning role played by broadcasting companies in more
recent years has been called post-fordist. The post-fordism of commissioning programmes suggests
small, quick turn-around, flexible and efficient. Although there may be some truth in this, it is often far
from the truth.   **29** What is meant by an 'integrated-factory' approach is that all aspects of the
programme from production to broadcasting is done within the one organisation – in a sense this is
analogous to the assembly-line factory production of Fordism.   **30** J. Tunstall, *Television producers*
(London: Routledge, 1993), p. 6.   **31** K. Robbins and J. Cornford, 'What is "flexible" about independent producers?', *Screen* 32:2 (1992) pp. 92–3.

focused mostly on sports programmes, but went on to say that that was because TnaG asked for sports programmes.[32] This illustrates the limited independence of independent companies and one can infer that this particular company did not have much freedom to choose what it produced for TnaG.

Both TnaG and independent producers are exposed to market forces which insist on maximising the audience with the minimum of resources. Independent production fails to lead to the increased diversity heralded by many, 'because independent producers are subject, if anything, to an even harsher sense of economic and commercial pragmatism and survival given their dependence upon the commissioning organization and its resources'.[33] Part of this pragmatism involves popularising programmes (even documentaries and current affairs) through switching to a magazine format, having 'sexy' or well-known presenters and dealing with consumer, leisure and human-interest issues emotively, in brief segments. Before coming on air TnaG encouraged 'popularised' programmes, an issue on which it was criticised – its promotional video aimed at young people was condemned, 'at least one teacher threw it in the bin, perturbed at the level of sexual innuendo and skin on the screen',[34] and its programmes in general have been criticised by Donncha Ó hÉalaithe for appealing to an urban audience and neglecting the Gaeltacht.[35] Cottle argued that 'such programme strategies for survival, then, while pointing to something of the creative responses of programme producers, nonetheless point to just that responses, not unfettered producer-driven creativity'.[36]

Producers visualise the audience at the most concrete level. They make particular programmes which have to appeal to a particular audience. Producers have a number of sources of information about their audience (or more to the point: how their programme is received). They can have access to audience ratings, they usually receive letters from viewers, they read press reports and the commissioning editor or the controller gives them 'feedback'. While the practical considerations of the broadcaster restrain the freedom of the producer to visualise the audience in the broadest sense, this is the point at which the audience is visualised at its most concrete. Decisions on content are usually predetermined by the practical considerations of the broadcaster, producers must include the content which they think will be most attractive to their audience, or in other words, attract the largest percentage of their potential audience. Producers are left with a limited autonomy concerning the exact content of their programmes.

Overall, because TnaG is subject to market forces and a limited budget, it must appeal to an audience larger than that provided by the Irish-speaking

32 P. Ó Ciardha, 1996, op. cit. **33** S. Cottle, 'Producer-driven television?', *Media, Culture and Society* 17 (1993), p. 1166. **34** J. Gogan, op. cit., p. 16. **35** Ibid. **36** S. Cottle, op. cit., p. 165.

community, which is reinforced by its publisher-broadcaster model which relies on independent producers who are subjected to the competition of the market (i.e. to achieve high ratings or be replaced by another independent producer). While appealing to a large audience corresponds with the market orientation of the 'modern' ideology, it contradicts their support for minority rights. Moreover. attracting a large audience to Irish-language programmes supports the opposing side of the dialectic.

TnaG – THE FIRST FEW YEARS

Before TnaG had started broadcasting Ó hÉalaithe was unhappy with the name and had attempted, unsuccessfully, to prevent the television channel being named TnaG by registering it for himself first. This attempt failed and TnaG began broadcasting in 1996 with a staff of 50; this increased to 60 over the next few years. During its first two months at the end of 1996 TnaG managed to attract 0.3% of the national audience. There was some conflict over ratings and TnaG refused to provide AC Nielsen with a programme schedule because it claimed that the ratings were incorrect – it pointed to occasions when it received higher ratings at night when it was off-air than for programmes during the day. The following year it more than doubled its audience share to 0.7%. By 1999 it had almost quadrupled its audience share to 1.1%. In 2000 it increased its share to 1.5% and again to 1.9% in 2001. (Source AC Nielsen www.medialive.ie). TnaG's own figures for 2000-1 are higher. It claims that its audience share increased from 1.9% in 2000 to 2.3% in 2001 and reaching 2.6% over Christmas 2001. It stated that it had almost achieved its objective of having a 3% share of the national audience. By early 2000, according to Horgan, TnaG had achieved a daily audience of 500,000.[37] This had increased to 730,000 two years later.[38]

TnaG began by broadcasting three hours in Irish every day, one of which it received from RTÉ. By 2002 it had increased this to five hours a day in Irish (while still receiving one hour of this from RTÉ) and a total of sixteen hours of broadcasting a day. It claims that it spends £15 million a year on programmes in Irish and that it creates 350 jobs.

During 1999 TnaG relaunched itself as TG4. It may be that the name TnaG was too similar to RnaG and suggested a local community Gaeltacht channel. The new name TG4 may also have been meant to reposition the channel in the Irish market, after the arrival of the commercial station TV3, in the way Channel4 is positioned in the UK market. One may wonder if the

37 J. Horgan, op. cit., p. 181.   38 www.tg4.ie

channel should have been named TG3 in the first place, in an attempt to deprive the commercial station of the claimed position, even if it could not secure the third position on the 'dial'.

TG4 is faced with a number of contradictory and conflicting forces through which it must manoeuvre. Paradoxical ideological demands are being made on TG4 to provide Irish speakers and non-Irish speakers with a public service and entertainment. Ideology is about how particular ideas and ways of behaving support particular positions of power. In modern Ireland one can discern two contradictory ideologies battling it out, each, in its turn, influencing the ideas and behaviour of those who created and those who run TG4. Thus, TG4 must manoeuvre between these contradictory social forces, these ideologies.

To a certain extent TG4 is protected from these forces by being under the umbrella of RTÉ (for the moment, at least), receiving 365 hours of programmes in Irish from RTÉ each year (at no cost to TG4) and by being funded by the State. However, the long-awaited Broadcasting Act (2001) has made it possible for TG4 to be separated from RTÉ. Also, this Act has not specified how TG4 will be funded into the future. Therefore it is possible that TG4 will be left to face the full force of market forces.

CONCLUSION

After independence, the ideological situation was one of nation-building. There was a continuation of the Irish nationalist ideology of pre-independence Ireland (late nineteenth-century and early twentieth-century). With the founding of the state, the discourse on the Irish language was central to national identity, supported by rural conservative traditional intellectuals. Initially, broadcasting, as well as the Irish language and Irish-language broadcasting, were elements of the ideology which was being employed in this nation-building project. The importance of the Irish language was manifested in various state activities, especially radio. During the first few decades the state held the reins of broadcasting. The programmes which were broadcast reflected the ideological efforts of the state to promote a particular national identity, and the discourse on the Irish language had been supported by its ideological position. Although financial concerns impacted a great deal on radio in this period, the aim was to provide a public service within these financial limitations and there was an expectation that a separate Gaeltacht radio channel could be established. The percentage of programmes in Irish, although quite low initially on 2RN, began to increase steadily on RÉ in the 1930s–50s.

By the time Irish television (RTÉ) was introduced in the 1960s an ideological offensive had been launched by intellectuals who emphasised the praxis of market forces, individualism and industrialisation, and de-emphasised the national narrative, including the Irish language. This ideological offensive came in the 1950s and 1960s in the form of a new ideology which '… accommodates itself to the form of the so-called consumer culture and fulfils, on a deeper level of consciousness, its old function, exerting pressure toward conformity with existing conditions'.[39] These two Irish ideologies have continued to exist concurrently, forming a dialectic from which no synthesis has emerged.

Economics was at the heart of the new ideology of convergence. On the European scale this was reflected in efforts to converge economically before embarking on cultural or even political issues. In Ireland this was reflected in the closing economic gap between north and south and cross-border cooperation.[40] On RTÉ this was reflected in increased reliance on advertising (in 1963 income from television advertising was higher than income from television licences).[41] During the debates about television, in 1960, Senator George O'Brien claimed that 'advertising has a definite commercial value in that it makes competition more keen. The more successful products tend to supplant the less successful …'[42] However, the result is that the majority is catered for to the neglect of minorities. A conflict ensues between the 'will of the majority', supported by the liberal ideology, and 'previously revered types of programmes', supported by the traditional ideology of distinctiveness.

This was a time when for the previous few decades as much as 10% of all airtime in Ireland was in Irish and it was hard to avoid hearing programmes in Irish. Within the modern ideology, however, the market gained dominance over identity. The new role of the market was reflected in the importance given to ratings. The ideological position of the discourse on the Irish language began to be challenged and gradually, as more choice became available, it became easier, for those who chose, to avoid programmes in Irish. It appeared after 1962 that perhaps, given a few years, the percentage of programmes in Irish on Telefís Éireann would begin to increase. Although the percentage did increase during the 1960s, it decreased dramatically from in the 1970s.

With the emergence of the centrality of ratings, the Irish language became a minority issue. With this recognition came demands for minority rights. The rights philosophy was used by the Gaeltacht civil rights movement which was part of the process that led to the emergence of Raidió na Gaeltachta. However, with the outbreak of violence in Northern Ireland

39 J. Habermas, 1989, op. cit., p. 215.   **40** L. O'Dowd, op. cit., p. 33.   **41** L. Doolan et al., op. cit., p. 36.   **42** Quoted in ibid., p. 16.

nationalism began to be attacked by those who articulated the ideology of modernisation. One result of this attack was the effort to restrict RnaG to the Gaeltacht.

During the decade that led to RnaG there was dissatisfaction with the small number of programmes in Irish on television. As early as 1964 there was a picket outside RTÉ, organised by the Universities' Gaelic Society, to protest against the scarcity of Irish-language programmes on RTÉ. During the 1970s and 1980s several reports were commissioned on Irish-language broadcasting and the findings ignored.

By the 1980s the modern ideology was faced with its failure in the form of a failing economy and the Northern troubles. This led to an ideological shift to a more neoliberal perspective, which was a more extreme version of the modern ideology. At this stage pressure began to mount from groups demanding the minority right to have a separate Irish-language channel. At around the same time as Conradh na Gaeilge's national convention, and in the same region (Connemara Gaeltacht), a Gaeltacht movement for a separate Irish-language television channel emerged. The single-issue groups which emerged in the Gaeltacht during the 1980s demanded a Gaeltacht channel, but by the late 1980s the Gaeltacht group and more national groups merged to form FNT and demanded an Irish-language channel for the whole of Ireland.

Teilifís na Gaeilge was the result of these demands. Although TG4 was presented by politicians and Irish-language organisations as a minority right, it is subject to market forces in the form of competition for a national audience and for advertising revenue. In this context TG4 today provides popularised programmes, emphasises drama and provides English-language subtitles in an attempt to attract as large an audience as possible to entice advertisers. While RTÉ was accused of neglecting Irish-language programming because of the market, TG4 is forced to structure the schedule around market forces in providing Irish-language programmes.

Broadcasting in Irish has had to navigate between two opposing ideologies. Each ideology promotes its own nexus of ideas and ways of behaving. The traditional ideology supports the promotion and restoration of Irish – two difficult and, to some extent, contradictory demands in themselves. However, the modern liberal-neoliberal ideology makes further demands – it expects commercial viability. In broadcasting, this implies raising finances via advertising revenue and directs attention toward attracting a large audience to gain the ratings required by advertisers. Nonetheless, one must not forget that rights are a central component of the liberal philosophy. This adds a further component – Irish speakers have a right to be informed and entertained in Irish.

In support of the small viewership, the traditional ideology emphasises the importance of preserving the language where it is spoken. Thus the emphasis is on a service purely for Irish speakers as is the case for RnaG and perhaps going so far as to support a 'community television' approach as well. RnaG relies wholly on RTÉ for funding and although RnaG is expected to compete for a 'reasonable' share of the Gaeltacht listenership to justify its existence, it is not expected to do battle in the commercial market for advertising revenue. This situation is quite similar for TG4 insofar as it is dependent on the state for about two-thirds of its income and on RTÉ for most of the rest in the form of technical support and one hour of programmes per day. However, TG4 is a national, rather than Gaeltacht, channel and it has undertaken to attract advertising revenue.

RTÉ is the most vulnerable to the conflict between the traditional and the (neo)liberal ideology. RTÉ continues to be a commercial station in competition with others while simultaneously being expected to fulfil public service obligations, including obligations to the Irish language. RTÉ scrambles to attract the largest possible audiences to obtain advertising revenue. As well as broadcasting programmes in Irish on RTÉ1, Network2 and Radio1, most of RTÉ's work for Irish is in its funding of RnaG and its support of TG4.

Programmes in Irish continue to fulfil several incongruous roles. These roles aim to accomplish two basic objectives – first, to promote and teach Irish amongst those who do not speak it, and, second, to preserve Irish where it is spoken and provide an Irish-language television service for Irish speakers. The emphasis on radio in the early years tended toward the former and, with the emergence of RnaG, Raidió na Life and TG4 the emphasis has tended toward the latter. Nonetheless, there are continuing efforts to promote Irish, albeit in a less compulsory and more individualised manner, and simultaneously there is a fear of ghetto-ising the language.

The Irish language has continued to hold an important position in Irish people's sense of national identity according to surveys and recent censuses, and attitudes to the language have become increasingly positive. Meanwhile the fear that the moderation of the more compulsory aspects of Irish on radio and television and in the education system would lead to a deterioration in the fortunes of the language have proved false (thus far at least). Irish has made inroads into the education and broadcasting systems in recent years in a more individualised and optional manner in the provision of more all-Irish schools, to which parents could choose to send their children, and in the provision of choice in the form of separate radio and television channels in Irish.

Appendices

Appendix 1. Letter from the Department of Posts and Telegraphs to the Department of the Taoiseach on the question of a special station for broadcasting in Irish, 30 October 1945[1]

30 October 1945

A Thaoisigh, A Chara,

You will remember raising the question of using the Radio more effectively for the development of the Irish language and culture and suggesting, among other things, that a Station might be provided which would broadcast solely in Irish so that persons in any part of the country interested in listening to Irish programmes could do so by tuning in to a Station from which nothing in the English language would be transmitted. The subject has been given very close examination here, both Departmentally and by means of a Committee composed of the officers principally concerned with broadcasting, all of whom are, incidentally, language enthusiasts. I am enclosing a copy of the Committee's report so that you may read it at your convenience.

The report, apart from its primary conclusions that an All-Irish Station would not be likely to increase appreciably the listening public for Irish programmes and that increased facilities for listening in the Gaeltacht are likely to have an injurious effect on the position of the Irish language in those areas, indicates that serious engineering and wavelength difficulties exist which appear to be insoluble in present circumstances. I had thought that a system of frequency–modulated stations distributed over the country would secure satisfactory reception in all parts but this type of transmission is, I am informed, still in the experimental stage and the special receivers required to receive programmes from such stations are not being manufactured on a commercial scale. The cost of a service of this sort would moreover be very considerable for apart from the cost of erecting the necessary number of stations, a heavy burden would inevitably fall on the station in respect of the supply of receivers. I imagine that we would have to make a present of the receivers to people, particularly in the Gaeltacht, if, as would be the case, they could only get the local frequency-modulated station on them.

The provision of a select programme for Gaeltacht listeners would not be easy for I understand that so far as speech features are concerned every dialect would have to be specially catered for and this could in present circumstances be done only to a very limited extent and at considerable cost. The reasoning in paragraphs 6 and 7 of the report are interesting in this connection.

1 DT S13756A. Published here with the permission of the Director of the National Archives of Ireland.

129

However, I think you will find that the report contains some very valuable recommendations of a positive character and, with your approval, I propose to direct the Department to follow them up. In particular the appointment of trained organisers fully equipped with the best modern recording apparatus (paragraphs 17–19 of the report) should introduce a 'real life' element into the programmes that is now often missing: indeed the taking of more outside broadcasts from country districts as a whole in Irish and English is something I had contemplated having done as soon as the necessary money and supplies became available.

Again, I am very much taken by the suggestion that Radio Éireann should have on its staff a team of Script Writers and a standing company of Producers and Actors capable of work of the highest competence in all the dialects of the Irish language.

I believe that with these two projects in operation, and with some effort on the part of popular bodies like Comhdhail Naisiunta na Gaeilge to organise group listening in the Gaeltacht, good work for the language and Irish culture generally could be done without harm to the language position in the Gaeltacht itself. When sets become plentiful the Gaeltacht people will get them inevitably either by purchase or second-hand from their friends and relations overseas; so that our immediate aim should be to educate them as far as possible to use the sets intelligently. I would hate to see the sets used, as gramophones were used formerly in the Gaeltacht, for purveying musical trash.

I think we should proceed to deal with the problem in the following order, because it is the order in which the material is available:

1. The establishment of a special staff of script writers in Irish and a special staff of speakers, announcers and actors.
2. An effort to get outside bodies to form listening groups in the Gaeltacht.
3. When available, to get a recording van to take local recordings. This will require organisers.
4. A very close eye on Frequency-Modulation development to be directed especially to receiving sets to be placed in schools and used for Gaelic cultural groups. Frequency-Modulated Gaelic programmes to be dovetailed into Radio Éireann programmes so as to give only Gaelic and Music to the Gaeltacht.

The plans for the new Broadcasting House in Exchequer Street are being delayed to some extent by the absence of a decision regarding the All Irish Station. I would, therefore, welcome an expression of your views on the subject as soon as you can find time to do so.

Yours sincerely,

P.J. Little

P.S. I don't know whether there is anything Radio Éireann could do to introduce a uniform mode of Irish speaking which would aim at being understood by all dialect speakers. This is a question on which you may have views.

Appendix 2. Report of the Departmental Committee to consider the question of special station/stations for broadcasting in Irish, 8 August 1945[2]

An Rúinaí,

1. On the 21st September, 1943, the Taoiseach discussed with the Secretary, Assistant Secretary and Director of Broadcasting the question of using the radio more effectively for the development of the Irish language and culture. He suggested the provision of a station which would broadcast solely in Irish so that persons whether in the Gaeltacht or Galltacht interested in listening to Irish programmes might be in a position for a reasonable time each day to tune in to a station from which there would be no non-Irish transmissions.

2. The Taoiseach wished residents in the Gaeltacht to be encouraged to listen to Irish radio programmes and suggested that cheap wireless sets – perhaps crystal sets – might be made available to them or, alternatively, some remission of the wireless licence fee might be given. He asked that the matter be examined and plans prepared so far as it was possible to do so in order that when circumstances admitted of the erection of a station, matters of staffing, programme schemes, etc. would be in a forward state of preparation. On the technical side, from discussions he had had with experts, he thought that it might be found that a series of low power stations, each serving a limited area, might be best for transmission.

3. The proposal was considered departmentally in the first instance and subsequently you appointed us a Committee with Mr S.S. Ó Floinn (Secretary's Office) as Secretary, in order to ensure a fuller examination of the subject.

4. Before examining in detail the problems involved in the provision of an all Irish Broadcasting Programme we felt we were not precluded from considering how much such a programme, if provided, would be likely to contribute to the development of the Irish language and Irish culture.

5. The first question that obviously arose in this connection was whether many people – with or without the stimulus of a State subsidy in the form of cheap sets or reduced licence fees – would listen to the programme, and this led us to enquire by means of a questionnaire addressed to Fior-Ghaeltacht Sub-Postmasters, the extent to which wireless is used at all in the Fior-Ghaeltacht, and the interest taken in the present programmes in Irish. The information thus obtained is summarised in Appendix A to this Report. It shows that approximately 10% of houses in the rural areas of the Fior-Ghaeltacht have wireless sets and that programmes in Irish are listened to in comparatively few of these houses. As in other parts of Ireland, a good deal of group listening takes place in the Gaeltacht, that is to say, that neighbours gather into houses that have sets to hear popular programmes, but, whether listened to by members of one or more households, it is an interesting fact that the programmes popular in the Gaeltacht are those that are most attractive

---

2 DT S13756A. Published here with the permission of the Director of the National Archives of Ireland.

everywhere in the country, namely English language features such as the News in English, Sports broadcasts, Question Time and Round the Fire. The news in Irish is not listened to by very many and by scarcely any when broadcast in a dialect other than their own.

6. This information substantially confirms our own observations. Wireless sets are still fairly rare in the Gaeltacht: so rare indeed as to emphasise the isolation which probably more than anything else has preserved Irish in those areas. Wireless can, however, be a potent means of spreading a knowledge of English, particularly among people anxious to learn it, and it is still unfortunately true that English has a fatal attraction for the Gaeltacht Dweller who is very seldom an enthusiast for the Irish language. This means that when he has a wireless set and can choose between programmes in Irish and English, he is not predisposed to choose Irish because it is Irish. If he does not exercise an absolute preference for English he does what the average listener everywhere does, i.e. he chooses the programme which in content and presentation is most likely to entertain him. In present circumstances, that is more likely to be a programme in English because these are far better served by script-writers, producers, actors, and by the common life of the country and the world, and consequently outpace, on the whole, the programmes in Irish – being more varied in subject, better written, more spontaneous, in the sense that they derive immediately from the activities which they report or interpret.

7. It might be argued that since the resident native speaker's knowledge of English is seldom very wide, he would find the difficulties of following English language broadcasts a deterrent; but it is, in our experience a fact that his difficulty in following a dialect other than his own is a much stronger deterrent to listening to programmes in Irish. The explanation would appear to be that the native speaker is accustomed to finding English difficult but attractive and is, therefore, content to make the effort; while being already proficient in one dialect of Irish, he is impatient and suspicious of other dialects and sees no reason why he should trouble himself to acquire a knowledge of them.

8. Following this line of thought, we desire to sound a note of warning as to the probable effect of a drive to make the Gaeltacht resident radio-conscious, especially if it takes the form of distributing cheap receiving sets. This might well be the reverse of what is desired by the Government, for increased listening in the Gaeltacht in the light of the present preference for programmes in English and the lower standard which must be accepted if additional programmes in Irish are to be provided – a matter that is discussed in detail later in this Report – is likely to cause the Gaeltacht resident to speak more English than he does now. He will certainly hear and understand more than he does now and from that to speaking English habitually will be an easy progression.

9. We considered a comparable enquiry in the Galltacht unnecessary and unlikely to yield results of any value. From our own wide experience, personal and official, we believe that programmes in Irish are more extensively listened to in those areas than in the Gaeltacht, but we also believe that the volume of programmes in Irish

from Radio Éireann is in existing circumstances quite adequate. In any event these programmes are not all as widely supported as we might expect, even by the enthusiast who theoretically is the sort of person who should benefit most from an increased radio ration of Irish. He will, of course, praise the project and welcome it in public, but it is in the highest degree improbable that he will actually hear more of the programmes in Irish continuously. The enthusiastic and proficient learner makes a greater initial effort to support programmes in Irish, but he has his own difficulties in maintaining the effort and he shares, very often, the prejudices of the native speaker in favour of the dialect which he knows best himself. It is unusual, outside Dublin, where the three dialects meet frequently, to find such wholehearted acceptance of all the dialects as will induce learners to perfect their understanding of them. Without going into any greater detail we may say that it is our experience that the enthusiastic learner is already almost as well served as, on the one hand, the talent available, and, on the other hand, his own energy in listening, make possible. (The word 'almost' implies the reservation that, given a standing company of actors and a team of script writers, the availability of talent could be greatly increased).

10. While the probable results of the provision of an all-Gaelic station would not, in our view, justify pursuance of the proposal, we have thought it desirable to examine in detail the problems involved in establishing the new station and programme.

Engineering Requirements

11. As regards transmission the aim should be to ensure that the programmes of an all-Irish station would be received satisfactorily in all parts of the country. Subject to the practical difficulties mentioned below this aim, we are advised by the Engineer-in-Chief, could be achieved in three ways –

   (i)   By providing a single High Power Station of at least 100 k.w. rating, estimated to cost £100,000 plus Customs charges. To obtain clear and satisfactory reception this Station would require an exclusive wavelength well removed from the wavelengths of Athlone and British Stations. It can be taken as definite that there is scarcely any prospect of obtaining such a wavelength. The present Athlone wavelength (531 metres) was obtained, after a long and difficult struggle, on the plea that this country is entitled to have one station capable of reaching the whole country. Even after this wavelength had been allocated by an International Convention difficulties were experienced because of interference by the Lithuanian Station, Klapeida; and at the last International Conference held at Montreux, Switzerland, early in 1939, Ireland notwithstanding the protests of our representatives, was called upon to share a wavelength with a Station in Palestine. The plan set up by this Conference was not brought into actual operation due to the outbreak of the war.

   The Dublin and Cork station wavelengths (222 and 241 metres respectively) are by international agreement shared with other stations and the use of power greater than 2 k.w. is forbidden by the agreement. Apart from the prohibition contained in the agreement it would not be practicable to serve the country from a central High Power Station using either of these wavelengths. Owing to technical problems of transmission on such wavelengths the outlying Gaeltacht areas in Donegal and Kerry would receive only a weak signal by daylight, and after dark would be subject to severe fading and interference from foreign stations sharing the wavelength.

(ii) By erecting a large number of stations with power of the order of that of the existing Dublin and Cork Stations (1¹/2 k.w.). Forty or more such stations and at least eight wavelengths would be required to cover the country. The difficulty of getting wavelengths has already been mentioned.

Even to serve only the Gaeltacht areas of Connaught, Donegal, Kerry and the Decies (Waterford) would involve the erection of 10 such stations at a cost of approximately £100,000 plus Customs charges. This cost as well as the other estimated Engineering costs cannot be very accurate as the level of postwar to pre-war prices has not as yet become clear.

(iii) By a system of frequency-modulated stations distributed over the country. This type of transmission has been in operation on an experimental basis for some time in the U.S.A. Frequency-modulated stations operate on the ultra-short wavelengths and their range is restricted more or less to 'optical paths', i.e., their range is that covered by what is termed 'line of sight'. The adoption of the frequency-modulated system of transmission would involve the erection of at least 10 stations and the cost would be approximately £100,000 plus Customs charges. However, there is the difficulty that special receivers of a type not at present manufactured on a commercial scale would be required to receive these transmissions.

To serve the Gaeltacht alone by these means would require at least four frequency-modulated stations.

12. Particulars of engineering staff required and the cost are given in Appendix B. It should be mentioned that it has been found difficult in the past to obtain suitable men with the necessary technical qualifications who could be trained for the engineering posts at the Broadcasting Stations. Experience also shows that there is little prospect of obtaining staffs with an adequate knowledge of Irish for an all-Irish Radio Station.

Question of Supplying Receivers

13. The Engineer-in-Chief has informed us that cheap and simple receiving sets will give good reception only in areas where the transmitting station can give a strong signal capable of over-coming interference from other stations, and a number of relatively high power transmitters would be required to fulfil this requirement. In the greater part of the Gaeltacht an electricity supply is not available and battery operated sets would have to be used. It is thought that a commercial battery receiver of the four valve type would represent the cheapest type likely to be avail-

able, and the cost of such a set would be about £10–£12. Maintenance costs such as battery charging, replacement of batteries, etc. would be from £2–£3 per annum.

14. If listening in the Gaeltacht is to be encouraged, the best course would be to reduce the initial cost of receivers by remitting the customs duty. This concession would have to be applied to the whole country.

15. The provision of crystal sets, even if they gave satisfactory reception, would not satisfy listeners because of poor reception, and because each listener would be isolated, and current comment and discussion impossible.

Programmes

16. For the purpose of considering the volume of programme material which would have to be provided it has been assumed that the broadcasts from the new station would be from 6 p.m. to 11 p.m. daily. The experience of Radio Éireann shows that there would be the greatest difficulty in securing suitable material for the additional programmes in Irish. Even granted unlimited financial resources the paucity of talent sets a definite limit to the volume of suitable material. The existing programme is only obtained in part from material offered; most of the time is filled by encouraging the few available people with any ability and understanding of the requirements of radio and supplying them with ideas.

17. Hitherto efforts within the Station's resources to obtain suitable material from I the Gaeltacht have met with little success and if the new station is to subserve the Gaeltacht primarily it will be necessary to provide a more specialised and elaborate organisation. Even with this we fear that the restricted life of the Gaeltacht will greatly limit the amount of broadcast material that can be taken direct therefrom and the standard of performance will inevitably be low. To achieve anything at all, it would be necessary to have in each of the three principal Gaeltacht areas a highly-trained organiser with mobile recording equipment whose duties would be to record or arrange for relays of occasional local events such as feiseanna, currach races, patterns, fairs, etc. and to seek out, test and encourage singers, instrumentalists, etc. Broadcasts of school choirs might be arranged and the seanchaidhthe induced to record their stories. A rural 'Brains Trust' dealing with occupational questions might in time be organised and matter procured for Talks of an informative and racy kind. It would be essential to have an efficient recording system as little of the Gaeltacht material could be broadcast direct.

18. In addition to salary and travelling expenses the organisers should receive allowances for other necessary 'out of pocket' expenses.

19. Some of the material collected by the Folklore Commission in the Gaeltacht areas might provide a basis for talks and dramatic features. The Commission's records could be examined and suitable material extracted. Consultation with the B.B.C. organiser of Scottish Gaeltacht programmes would, in our view, also be most useful in connection with the building of programmes from Gaeltacht material.

20. The lack of programme material, in our opinion, rules out the possibility of providing a separate programme for each of the larger Gaeltacht areas or provinces and we, therefore, do not think it necessary to express any view as to whether it would be desirable to have three such programmes. There is no doubt however, that the dialect difficulty is a serious one and would have to be constantly kept in mind in framing programmes. It would be desirable to give each dialect an equitable proportion of time and in publishing the programmes the dialect to be used in each feature would need to be indicated.

21. In view of the dearth of programme material as many as possible of Radio Éireann's Irish programmes would have to be relayed by the proposed new station if it were to broadcast for S hours daily. On examination of Radio Éireann's current programmes it has been found that approximately 12 hours 40 minutes per week of programmes in Irish could be relayed by the new station.

22. Programmes, apart from relays from Radio Éireann, would then have to be provided from the new station for 22 hours 20 minutes weekly on average. In order to provide a properly balanced programme, allowance being made for the items which would be relayed, this time could be divided approximately as follows:

Music		News		Talks, Prose, Poetry, Stories, etc.		Plays and Drama		Commentaries		Total	
H.	M.	H.	M.	H.	M.	H.	M.	H.	M.	H.	M.
9	45	4	35	6	20	1	30		10	22	20

23. *Music.* A permanent station combination would be required which would broadcast for a total of a little over 4 hours per week and an Octet would best serve the purpose. Records would occupy about 2 hours and the balance of 3 1/2 hours, approximately would be taken up by singers and instrumentalists engaged as required.

24. *News.* It is contemplated that the News broadcasts would usually be Irish versions of the news as broadcast in English from Radio Éireann and would be broadcast at the same times as the News in English. Whether this arrangement should be adopted is a matter that would require further consideration if it were decided to proceed with the proposal for a new station. On the assumption that the news broadcasts would be on these lines an Assistant Editor and two Reporters would, we estimate, be required for the preparation of the News in Irish.

25. *Special Programmes.* As already stated, the greatest difficulty is experienced in securing the comparatively small number of talks, plays, etc. in Irish at present broadcast from Radio Éireann and it is quite clear that the few writers who are able and willing to write scripts for the radio are already fully occupied. The volume of material required for the new station could be provided only by employing a full-time staff of Script writers who would have to be specially trained. Five Script writers would, we calculate, be necessary to produce between them finished scripts for about 5 1/2 hours programmes per week. Their work would include, in addition to original articles, stories, documentaries, etc. translations of suitable

English and European plays and stories. As competent people would be most likely to be already in secure positions it would be necessary to offer an attractive salary to induce them to take up radio work.

26. What has been said regarding the difficulty of obtaining sufficient scripts applies also to the production and acting of plays, dramatisations, etc. and it would be essential to engage a whole-time Producer, Assistant Producer and a standing company of 10 actors for the purposes of the new Station's programmes. The actors would need to be carefully selected and trained for acting 'on the air'. Their training should be directed specially to attainment of versatility in the different dialects. It is contemplated that in addition to taking parts in plays, etc., they would be employed as expert readers of stories and talks. Their services could be availed of to some extent in the Radio Éireann programmes also and would be very valuable for this purpose. Indeed the establishment of a standing company of actors and appointment of Staff Script writers may be regarded as necessary apart altogether from the question of a new all Irish programme if Radio Éireann's present Irish programmes are to be brought to as high a standard as productions in English. At present the Director has to depend upon the part-time services of a very limited number of amateur writers and actors – mainly Civil Servants, Teachers and the like – with the result that it is almost impossible to secure suitable scripts, sufficient rehearsal or really effective production of Irish features. While we recognise that it is perhaps somewhat beyond our terms of reference we think it well to place on record our opinion that a standing company of actors and a staff of script writers should be engaged for the purpose of Radio Éireann's Irish programmes.

27. *Announcers.* Three Announcers would be required for the new station.

General direction of new Station

28. The Committee consider that it would be necessary to appoint two Assistant Directors, one for Radio Éireann and one for the new station. Both stations would be under the general control of the Director and Deputy Director, the Deputy Director to preside over the programme conferences of both.

29. An additional Assistant Music Director responsible to the Music Director would be required to take direct charge of music programmes of the new station.

30. The broadcasting of a greater quantity of spoken Irish would be the real *raison d'etre* of the Gaelic station.

In Radio Éireann most Gaelic programmes are under the direction of the Talks Officer and the assistant to the Talks Officer the only exceptions are: programmes for children and predominantly musical features.

In addition, these two officers control several types of English speech programmes, solo talks, short stories, discussions, poetry, documentaries, etc.

The Committee considers that the programme officer most suitable to be entrusted with the general direction of all programmes of spoken Irish would be the Radio Éireann Talks Officer. This officer would continue to be generally responsible for the Radio Éireann programmes which he at present directs but the increased range of his duties would necessitate other appointments; and the duties themselves would be of a much more general character, day-to-day routine and detail being, as far as possible, the concern of his staff.

This staff, in our view, should in addition to the Talks Officer's Assistant, consist of:

(1) A Deputy Talks Officer for Radio Éireann programmes;

(2) Another Deputy Talks Officer for Gaelic Station programmes;

(3) The five script writers, Producer, Assistant Producer, Producer and Station actors referred to above.

31. In view of the increased announcing staff which would be employed and the difficulties inevitable in securing that exact timing which would be an essential part of the system of relaying programmes as proposed, we consider that a Studio Supervisor should be appointed who would supervise the Announcers and be on duty during broadcasting hours to give all necessary instructions as to items to be 'cut' etc.

32. Additional Clerical staff, typists and messengers, as well as Office accommodation and equipment, would also be required.

33. A staff plan showing the proposed broadcasting organisation is at Appendix C.

Cost of Proposals

34. A statement is attached (Appendix B) showing the estimated cost under various headings of the arrangements visualised in this report. The estimates given of salaries for some of the posts proposed, e.g. script writers, are of necessity highly speculative. No provision has been made for extra remuneration to the Director, Deputy Director, Music Director or Talks Officer whose duties and responsibilities would be substantially enlarged. We are of opinion, nevertheless, that the figure of total estimated annual cost may be relied upon as a reasonably close estimate.

35. Very heavy expense would have to be incurred in providing the studios and staff accommodation required for the new station but as the preparation of any reliable estimate would take much time we think it better that it be prepared Departmentally in order that submission of our report may not be delayed.

Conclusions

36. Our conclusions may be summarised as follows:

In present circumstances:

(1) an all-Irish Radio Station would not be likely to increase appreciably the listening public for Irish programmes either in the Gaeltacht or Galltacht;

(2) that increased facilities for listening in the Gaeltacht are likely to have an injurious effect on the position of the Irish language in those areas.

(3) As regards the Galltacht the Irish language cause can be advanced more effectively by the mixed English and Irish programme as given from Radio Éireann.

(4) A new Station could not be established whose transmissions would be heard effectively throughout the country unless a suitable wavelength free from interference were obtained; and there is no prospect of a suitable wavelength being obtained.

(5) A five hour programme daily, (incorporating the maximum amount of Irish speech and musical features from Radio Éireann) could be provided with great difficulty and at heavy cost

(6) The establishment of a standing company of actors and an appropriate staff of script-writers is regarded as necessary if Radio Éireann's present [small piece torn from document]

37. In concluding we wish to record our appreciation of the very capable assistance given by Mr S.S. Ó Floinn as Secretary to the Committee.

(Sgd) LEON O'BROIN Assistant Secretary. Chairman.

S. Ó BRAONÁIN Director of Broadcasting.

C. Ó CEALLAIGH Deputy Director of Broadcasting.

ROIBEÁRD Ó FARACHÁIN Talks Officer, Radio Éireann.

P.L. Ó COLMÁIN Assistant Principal Officer, Secretary's Office.

8 August 1945

Bibliography and sources

PERSONAL INTERVIEWS WITH THE AUTHOR

Higgins, Michael D., 4 June 1998.
Ó Briain, Colm, 26 November 1998.
Ó Ciardha, Pádhraic, 19 February 1996.
Ó Ciardha, Pádhraic, 11 June 1998.
Ó Feinneadha, Ciarán, 25 August 1998.
Ó Gadhra, Nollaig, 11 April 1997.
Ó hÉalaithe, Donncha, 11 April 1997.

BIBLIOGRAPHY

Advisory Planning Committee 1986, *The Irish language in a changing society: shaping the future*. Dublin: Bord na Gaeilge.
Andrews, Geoff 1991 (ed.), *Citizenship*. London: Lawrence and Wishart.
Barbrook, R. 1992, 'Broadcasting and national identity in Ireland', *Media, Culture and Society* 14: 203–27.
Baudrillard, Jean 1983, *In the shadow of the silent majorities*. New York: Semiotext(e).
Berg, M., P. Hemanus, J. Ekecrantz, F. Mortensen and P. Sepstrup 1997 (eds), *Current theories in Scandinavian mass communications research*. Greaa: GMT.
Bord na Gaeilge 1983, *Action plan for Irish 1983–6*. Dublin: Bord na Gacilge.
Browne, Donald R. 1992, 'Radio na Gaeltachta: swan song or preserver', *European journal of Communications* 7.
Calhoun, Craig 1993 (ed.), *Habermas and the public sphere*. London: MIT Press.
Cathcart, Rex 1984, 'Broadcasting – the early decades', pp. 39–50 in Brian Farrell (ed.), *Communications and community in Ireland*. Dublin: Mercier Press.
Clancy, P., M. Kelly, J. Wiatr and R. Zoltaniecki (eds) 1992, *Ireland and Poland: comparative perspectives*. Dublin: Department of Sociology, University College Dublin.
CLAR 1975, *Committee on Irish language attitudes research report*. Dublin: Government Stationery Office.
Coiste Comhairleach Pleanála 1986, *The Irish language in a changing society: shaping the future*. Baile Átha Cliath: Bord na Gacilge.
Commins, P. 1988, 'Socioeconomic development and language maintenance in the gaeltacht', *Language Planning in Ireland: International Journal of the Sociology of Language* 70: 11–28.
Cottle, Simon 1993, 'Producer-driven television?', *Media, Culture and Society*, 17: 159–66.

Department of Arts, Culture and the Gaeltacht 1995, *Active or passive? Broadcasting in the future tense: green paper on broadcasting*. Dublin: Government Stationery Office.

Doolan, Lelia, Jack Dowling and Bob Quinn 1969, *Sit down and be counted: the cultural evolution of a television station*. Dublin: Wellington Publishers.

Fahy, Tony 1989, 'Listenership up 10 Percent', *Irish Broadcasting Review* 8: 56–7.

Fennell, Desmond 1980, 'Can a shrinking linguistic minority be saved? Lessons from the Irish experience', in Einar Haugen et al. (eds), *Minority Languages Today*. Edinburgh: Edinburgh University Press.

Fianna Fáil and the Labour Party 1993, *Programme for partnership government 1993–7: fostering our language, culture and heritage: expanding bilingualism in Irish society: guidelines for action programmes in the state sector*.

Fine Gael, The Labour Party and Democratic Left 1994, *A government of renewal: a policy agreement between Fine gael, the Labour Party and Democratic Left*.

Fisher, Desmond 1978, *Broadcasting in Ireland*. London: Routledge and Kegan Paul.

Fishman, Joshua A. 1991, *Reversing language shift: theoretical and empirical foundations of assistance to threatened languages*. Clevedon: Multilingual Matters.

Gogan, Johnny 1996, 'Ar Aghaidh Linn', *Film Ireland* April/May.

Gorham, Maurice 1967, *Forty years of broadcasting*. Dublin: Talbot Press.

Gramsci, Antonio 1971, *Selections from the prison notebooks*. London: Lawrence and Wishart.

Habermas, Jürgen 1979, *Communication and the evolution of society*. London: Heinemann.

Habermas, Jürgen 1989, *The structural transformation of the public sphere*. Cambridge: Polity Press.

Habermas, Jürgen 1992, 'Citizenship and national identity: some reflections on the future of Europe', *Praxis International* 12(1): 1–19.

Harrison, M.L. 1991, 'Citizenship, consumption and rights: a comment on B.S. Turner's theory of citizenship', *Sociology* 25(2): 209–13.

Held, David 1991, 'Between State and civil society: citizenship', pp. 19–25 in Geoff Andrews (ed.), *Citizenship*. London: Lawrence and Wishart.

Heller, M., D. Nemedi and R. Rényi 1994, 'Structural changes in the Hungarian public sphere under State socialism', *Comparative Social Research* 14: 15771.

Hindley, Reg 1990, *The death of the Irish language*. London: Routledge.

Hobsbawm, Eric 1990, *Nations and nationalism since 1780*. Cambridge: Cambridge University Press.

Horgan, John 2001, *Irish media:a critical history since 1922*. London: Routledge.

Hourigan, Niamh 1998, 'Framing processes and the Celtic television campaigns', *Irish Journal of Sociology* 8: 49–70.

Hourigan, Niamh 2001, *Comparison of the campaigns for Raidió na Gaeltachta and TnaG*. Maynooth: Department of Sociology, National University of Ireland, Maynooth.

Kelly, Mary 1992, 'The media and national identity in Ireland', pp 75–90 in Patrick Clancy et al. (eds), *Ireland and Poland: comparative perspectives*. Dublin: Department of Sociology, University College Dublin.

Kelly, Mary and Bill Rolston 1995, 'Broadcasting in Ireland: issues of national identity and censorship', pp. 563–92 in P. Clancy et al. (eds), *Irish society: sociological perspectives*. Dublin: Institute of Public Administration.

Kirby, Peadar 1997, *Poverty amid plenty: world and Irish development reconsidered*. Dublin: Trócaire.

Lee, Joseph J. 1989, *Ireland 1912–85: politics and society*. Cambridge: Cambridge University Press.

Marshall, T.H. 1992, 'Citizenship and social class', in T.H. Marshall and Tom Bottomore, *Citizenship and social class*. London: Pluto Press.

O' Connor, Barbara 1983, *Irish language media: discussion document*. Dublin: Bord na Gaeilge.

O'Dowd, Liam 1992, 'State legitimacy and nationalism in Ireland', pp 25–42 in P. Clancy et al. (eds), *Ireland and Poland: comparative perspectives*. Dublin: Department of Sociology, University College Dublin.

Ó Feinneadha, Ciarán 1995, 'TnaG – an ród a bhí romhainn', *Combar* 54(5): 10–14.

Ó Gadhra, Nollaig 2001, 'The Gaeltacht and the future of Irish', *Studies* 90(360): 433–4.

Ó Glaisne, Risteard 1982, *Raidió na Gaeltachta*. Indreabhán: Cló Cois Fharraige.

Ó Riagáin, Pádraig 1988, 'Introduction', *Language planning in Ireland: International Journal of the Sociology of Language* 70: 5–9.

Ó Riagáin, Pádraig 1992, *Language maintenance and language shift as strategies of social reproduction: Irish in the Corca Dhuibhne Gaeltacht 1926–86*. Baile Átha Cliath: ITÉ.

Ó Riagáin, Pádraig and Mícheál Ó Gliasáin 1994, *National survey on languages 1993: preliminary report*. Dublin: ITÉ.

Oifig an tSoláthair 1993, *Daonáireamh 86, Imleabhar 5: An Ghaeilge*. Baile Átha Cliath: Oifig Dhíolta Foilseacháin Rialtais.

Peillon, Michel 1982, *Contemporary Irish society: an introduction*. Dublin: Gill and Macmillan.

Pine, Richard 2002, *2RN and the origins of Irish radio*. Dublin: Four Courts Press.

Quill, Tríona 1994, 'Television and the Irish language', *Irish Communications Review* 4: 6–17.

Robbins, Kevin and James Cornford 1992, 'What is "flexible" about independent producers?', *Screen* 32(2): 190–200.

RTÉ 1995, *RTÉ Response to the Government's Green Paper on broadcasting*. Dublin: RTÉ.

Thompson, John B. 1994, 'Ideology and modern culture', pp. 133–41 in A. Giddens, D. Held, D. Hubert, D. Seymore and J. Thompson (eds), *The polity reader in social theory*. Cambridge: Polity Press.

Thoreau, Henry David 1995, *Civil disobedience*. London: Penguin Books.

TnaG 1995, *Cén Fáth TnaG?* Dublin: TnaG.

TnaG 1995, *Páipéar Glas an Rialtais ar Chraolachán: Freagra Theilifís na Gaeilge*. Dublin: TnaG.

Tovey, Hillary, Damien Hannan and Hal Abramson 1989, *Why Irish? Irish identity and the Irish language*. Dublin: Bord na Gaeilge.

Tunstall, J. 1993, *Television producers*. London: Routledge.

Turner, Bryan S. 1990, 'Outline of a theory of citizenship', *Sociology* 24(2): 189–217.

Turner, Bryan S. 1991, 'Further specification of the citizenship concept: a reply to M.L. Harrison', *Sociology* 25(2): 215–18.

Watson, Iarfhlaith 1996, 'The Irish language and television: national identity, preservation, restoration and minority rights', *British Journal of Sociology* 47(2): 255–74.

Watson, Iarfhlaith 1997, 'A history of Irish language broadcasting: national ideology, commercial interest and minority rights', pp. 212–30 in Mary Kelly and Barbara O'Connor (eds) *Media audiences in Ireland: power and cultural identity*. Dublin: UCD Press.

Watson, Iarfhlaith 1997, 'Teilifís na Gaeilge as a public sphere', *Irish Communications Review* 7.

Watson, Iarfhlaith 1999, 'An Dá Thrá', *Combar* 58(4): 18–20.

Watson, Iarfhlaith 2001, 'TG4 Féiniúlacht agus Saoránacht', *Feasta* 54(7): 12–13.

Watson, Iarfhlaith 2001, 'TG4 Féiniúlacht agus Saoránacht', *Irish Journal of Sociology* 10(2): 1–12.

Watson, Iarfhlaith 2001, 'Stair an Chraolacháin Ghaeilge', *An t-Ultach* 78(6): 9–10.

Watson, Iarfhlaith 2002, 'Irish-language broadcasting: history, ideology and identity', *Media Culture & Society* 24(5): 1–19.

Webster, Andrew 1990, 2nd (ed.) *Introduction to the sociology of development*. London: Macmillan Press.

Working Group on Irish Language Television Broadcasting 1987, *Report to the Ministers for the Gaeltacht and Communications*. Dublin: Government Stationery Office.

Young, Iris Marion 1989, 'Polity and group difference: a critique of the ideal of universal citizenship', *Ethics* 99: 250–74.

Index